My Kid is Doing Drugs and Got Arrested: Now What?

A guide for parents and others who love
a teenage drug user.

Donna Beard Gilchrist MSN, WHP

T0104947

AuthorHouse™
1663 Liberty Drive
Bloomington, IN 47403
www.authorhouse.com
Phone: 1-800-839-8640

© *2013 by Donna Beard Gilchrist RN, MSN, WHNP-BC. All rights reserved.*

No part of this book may be reproduced, stored in a retrieval system, or transmitted by any means without the written permission of the author.

Published by AuthorHouse   03/15/2013

ISBN: 978-1-4817-2913-0 (sc)
ISBN: 978-1-4817-2912-3 (e)

Library of Congress Control Number: 2013904743

Any people depicted in stock imagery provided by Thinkstock are models, and such images are being used for illustrative purposes only.
Certain stock imagery © Thinkstock.

This book is printed on acid-free paper.

Because of the dynamic nature of the Internet, any web addresses or links contained in this book may have changed since publication and may no longer be valid. The views expressed in this work are solely those of the author and do not necessarily reflect the views of the publisher, and the publisher hereby disclaims any responsibility for them.

Medical Disclaimer

This book is not intended to prescribe treatment for substance abuse or mental illness. It is intended to give an overview of the options available to you with the hope that you will seek the help of health care professionals as you move towards recovery.

ENDORSEMENT by JOHN E. MARTIN, PhD.

Lost and Found:

The Fall and Rise of a Drug Addicted Son
- and the Collateral Damage, Learning Process and Greater Love Found
John E. Martin, Ph.D.

To the Family:

You don't have to use drugs to suffer from drug addiction
- *(adapted from AA slogan)*

To the Addict:

He who is often reproved, yet stiffens his neck,
will suddenly be broken beyond healing.
- *Proverbs 29:1 (ESV)*

As I read through this powerful book I found myself wondering: Is it a mother's book about a son, both challenged by his drug addiction, or is it a son's book as through the eyes of the mother who loves him? I'm still not entirely sure. But I decided it must be both.

There are three sides to any story and this one is no exception: There's the Person, in this case the addict, there's the Parent or Significant Other, in this case the book's author and 'chief sufferer,' and then there's the affected others, in this case the sister and father. I might say there is a significant 4th involved, in fact a very significant other – God. But this story is told from the perspective of the first three, and beautifully at that.

When asked to offer my thoughts and perspective on My Kid is Doing Drugs and Got Arrested: Now What? A guide for parents and others who love a teenage drug user by Donna Beard Gilchrist, I readily said yes. You should know that I happen to be a friend of the family, particularly the father and husband, Guy, and I've come to know both Donna and Matt during the several years he and I have been friends. In addition, Donna and I share the same book agent. Now that is not a very good reason for choosing me. Anyone who knows the family could write a reaction to a book about them. A better reason would be that, I am a professor and teacher of psychology, a licensed clinical psychologist, and an addictions treatment expert, with over 30 years specializing in research and intervention on addictive behavior.

Further, and perhaps unknown to Donna and Matt, I also know addiction from the inside as well. Thirty years ago I, too, struggled with life's unmanageability due to drinking, after having grown up in an alcoholic family, and I found myself renting chairs in AA and Alanon meetings over a couple year period. That's where I found God – or rather God found me. Matt's fall, struggle, and eventual rehabilitation and recovery was well described, including his neurochemical, behavioral, cognitive, and social restoration to health. What makes this wonderful book so compellingly readable, as well as so highly educational, is the fascinating interplay between Matt and Donna's stories, and her walking the reader gently through a reality course on the science of addiction – its types, findings, theories and treatments.

Ultimately, this well-written story powerfully invites the reader into their family home, and the surprise, unscheduled classroom on substance abuse and dependence, focused on Matt and what happened to him and those who love him.

I especially loved, as I believe the reader will as well, the probing and at times profound quotes by Matt, leading the reader into each new chapter topic, and his story epilogue at the end. It has a happy ending, as you might have figured out (sorry if I have spoiled the ending for you!). But it's the meat of this addiction story sandwich that has the real learning nutrition. The author, Donna, has done a creditable job in illustrating the various stages of the addiction cycle, from the early stresses and emotional traumas, to experimentation with substances that reduce or temporarily anesthetize the pain, that lead to the compulsive habit and social reconstruction around use, abuse to dependence. Her nice simplification of the neurochemistry – which can get awfully complicated – should be helpful to those many whose eyes glaze over when others try to explain what happens in the brain. And I was impressed with her broad attention to the various substances and addictive behaviors that have so damaged so many young minds, lives, and families.

The description of the various resources available to the family of the addict will be most useful to the reader, all the way from the excellent web-based government sources, such as NIH, NIDA, and SAMHSA, to the social community programs such as AA, NA and Alanon. Families fighting addiction need support, and lots of it, and this book is a testament to this important reality. The story of the rehabilitation and detox programs – both rejected and finally accepted – are also most interesting. I like that the author does not take the black or white, all or nothing perspective on relapse. She appropriately refers to it as a stage in final recovery. It's not a matter of whether addicts will relapse, but when and how they will react. This is not to say that relapse is a good thing. It's not. Prevention is best, and Donna does a nice job of presenting the various stimuli and triggers, as well as environmental conditions associated with relapse and substance abuse.

A long time ago I learned, and would teach my students, that we cannot and should not ever try to counsel a drug. We counsel people and families. Detox must come first, or we will be trying to negotiate with the drug, and drug states take over the brain. "Good luck" I would tell my therapy students, in trying to do therapy with a person who was high or in drug withdrawal to any extent. But when the drug and the individual's free choice are challenged head-on, and yet are still "married" together, as it were, "we have a problem, Houston." Yet, the author does a nice job of addressing this very issue. How did they use 'tough' but effective love to change Matt's mind? Unfortunately at times, such as with Matt, those 18 and over cannot be forced into treatment against their will, as Matt's story demonstrates so well. Donna's "NEVER GIVE UP" and KEEP TRYING (NO MATTER WHAT), is effectively communicated in her story of Matt and her struggles.

Though we can lead the horse to "water," we can't make it drink. We CAN, however, salt his oats, to make him more thirsty for the (healing) water we offer. This book shows one way, or rather many ways, how. But the bottom line is motivation, and Matt eventually was led, if not somewhat forcefully at times, into a new motivation. His epilogue at the end shows his new life, and new motivations that could not arise and be nourished so long as the drugs, and the overwhelming desire for "pleasureable" escape and avoidance, held it down in a death grip.

Along with the many excellent resources and suggestions for treatment that are provided in the book, there is an additional resource that has been born out of considerable research on the addictions. It is called motivational interviewing, and is now one of the treatments of choice for the addictions (see www.motivationalinter-view.org for more information and available treatment resources). Not surprisingly, this book offers a number of those effective approaches to motivation, albeit non-systematically, that work.

Do not conform to the pattern of this world but be transformed by the renewing of your mind. Then you will be able to test and approve what God's will is—his good, pleasing and perfect will. (Romans 12:2, NIV)

A final source of healing comes from God and His Spirit. AA knows this, the 12-Steps are built around spiritual and biblical truths (especially the book of James), and (surprise!) science agrees. Those with a strong spiritual and especially religious background, and practice (either before or during the addiction treatment), do far better in both avoiding severe addiction as well as in overall recovery, avoidance of relapse, and full healing and life change.

Lastly, I remember some years ago when my teenage nephew came to me with a problem. He was addicted to pain killers and amphetamines, has robbed a drug store in another state, and had been on the run from the law for some time. He asked what I thought he should do. I offered to intervene on his behalf with the judge of the court that he had refused to appear before. He agreed and gave me the name and address of the court and judge. So I called him and did what my nephew didn't expect but that I knew was necessary. I asked the judge what was the maximum sentence he could give him. I was told a year. I then asked the judge to give him the full year, but to make it at a drug facility. He did, and the rest is history. This all happened before California's institution of the Drug Courts for this very purpose: trading criminal time for rehab.

My nephew is now a proud dad and functional member of society. I think by now, years later, he has forgiven me for my part in all that. It was the same tough, but effective, love Donna and Guy finally gave to Matt. And I know that he is grateful, as this wonderful story so illustrates.

I would like to dedicate the following quote from the Bible to Donna, Guy, Megan, and especially the miracle Matt:

And we know that [a]God causes all things to work together for good
to those who love God,
to those who are called according to His purpose.
- Rom 8:28 (NASB)

TABLE of CONTENTS

DEDICATION

I dedicate this book to my awesome son, Matt. Matt, your story is compelling and inspirational. Your journey to recovery is amazing and I hope for only good things to happen to you in the future. Please hold on to the fragile gift of recovery. I know you can do it!

ACKNOWLEDGEMENTS

So many wonderful people have helped make his book a reality. A friend of my husband's recommended a Literary Agent who has worked with first time authors for over 15 yrs. The Wilcox Agency in Del Mar, California as someone who could help me put my book together, help me with advice on how to get it published and the best sources to use, as well as how to sell books. Ariela Wilcox has been instrumental in moving my work to publication.

My closest friends and family supported me through the horrible ordeal of Matt's addiction and then became my book advisors and helped me remember stories and feelings as I wrote my book. Many thanks and love to: Guy, Nancy, Marilyn, MaryAnn, Barbara, Marsha, Gary, Maria, Virginia, Jeevan, Jane, Nancy H., and Tammie.

Many thanks to David Davis - MCD Advertising & Design for taking Matt's picture and initial design and making it look so professional, as well as for the design of the Interior pages. David really listens and works hard to capture the vision in a writer's head and then brings it into reality. You couldn't choose a better designer for your book.

Thanks to Matt for allowing me to share his story with candor. Also thanks for the awesome cover art, "There is Hope" which you painted during a hopeful moment in your recovery. Thanks also for the artwork in the book which shows the terrible pain drug abuse causes. I think it shows your pain better than words could explain. I know you will make a great graphic designer when your college days are over.

Special thanks to Jaclyn who did a critical read of my earliest rough draft and offered editorial suggestions. A special thanks to Bradley Meier Ph.D. for validating that this work was accurate medically, the story important, and encouraging me to tell it like it was. Most of all, undying gratitude to Donna Ehlers MD and Mike Pearlman MFT, Matt's amazing mental health clinicians for helping Matt on his journey of recovery.

David Davis: MCD Advertising & Design:
PH: (310) 545.2233 | eMail: david@mcd-adv.com

Ariela Wilcox - The Wilcox Agency:
1155 Camino del Mar # 173 - Del Mar, Ca. 92014

FOREWARD

Bradley Meier Ph.D.
Licensed Clinical Psychologist

It is a pleasure to write the forward for **My Kid's Doing Drugs and Got Arrested; Now What?** It is one of those works that causes the reader to pause and question why such a book was never written; until now. This book captures one of our worse fears as a parent; proceeding through life and suddenly realizing that we don't have control over a central element of it despite our best intentions and efforts. **My Kid Is Doing Drugs** fills a void for parents who find themselves thrust into a world that seems far removed from day-to-day realities, and for others, who think they know that world but suddenly do not when it is happening to them.

The book beautifully highlights and captures the interplay between substance abuse and mental illness and the importance of addressing both. Perhaps more importantly, it implicitly recognizes that these challenges are life-long, even with stability; not just something that can be "fixed."

One aspect that I really liked about **My Kid Is Doing Drug**s is that it captures the reality of the emotions we can all identify with and only hope to imagine. It takes us through the stages of shock, despair and helplessness as well as shame, unrelenting fear and suspicion along with self-blame. It also describes beautifully the selective attention that leads to enabling, which is hard to understand when on the outside looking in, but eminently understandable when the reader puts him/herself in the mindset of the author. We all would like to believe that 'It will never happen to me' but can easily understand after reading this book how quickly our lives can turn. The simple message, "Listen to your inner voice," is critical in reducing denial in the short-term and guilt in the long-run.

While the human element of the book makes for an engaging read, it is also chock full of information and resources. It gives the reader insights about navigating jail, the importance of picking the right treatment, and outlines the physiology of addiction in a simple manner that would make a scientist proud. The author,

Donna Beard Gilchrist, provides the reader with very useful and readily applicable information such as early warning signs that are easily overlooked (i.e. denial), substance abuse trends and concise information about a full spectrum of intoxicants readily available to all. In addition, she provides references for lots and lots of resources so that the reader can continue to educate him/herself about mental health and substance abuse and make some very personal, informed decisions about what is right for his/her situation.

In total, **My Kid Is Doing Drugs** is a very personal and emotional story while also offering a plethora of practical information. The book clearly captures how "recovery is a fragile gift" worth fighting for and treasuring.

PART 1 - LIFE is NOT EASY

INTRODUCTION

"There are things in life we don't want to happen, but have to accept, things we don't want to know but have to learn. ANNON

Some say that life begins at the end of your comfort zone. Well my comfort zone ended on February 1, 2004. That is the day my son was arrested for drug possession and I was confronted with the reality that Matt is a drug addict. He was a tweeker (meth), junkie (heroin) and one messed up teenager! I began a journey that I never thought I would take. Since then I have learned never to say "that won't happen to me" because life has a funny way of proving us wrong.

Anyone looking at me would think I had a perfect life. I had been married for 20 years, had 2 great, talented kids, a very successful career as a Nurse Practitioner, a big supportive extended family, great friends, involved in a church community and lived in a nice neighborhood. I kept my kids involved in sports, music lessons, church groups and had a strong focus on their high school academics looking towards college. I supported the activities my kids participated in; I was a team mom, PTA officer, community volunteer for Campfire Girls and Boys and Boy Scouts. I thought that keeping my kids busy was a way of keeping them out of trouble. Boy was I wrong.

Growing up in the 1950's and 60's was very different than today. My family was a very close knit "Father Knows Best Family." Lots of love, involvement and parental encouragement fostered my athletic and academic success. I was the first in my family to graduate from college. This model was how I approached parenting.

I attended college in the late 60's and early 70's and was channeled into a traditional female major. I became a nurse and after 6 months I aspired to expand my role and became a nurse practitioner. I continued on and obtained a Masters Degree, had a busy OB-GYN practice with a large HMO in the Los Angeles area, and became a visiting faculty member at a local State College. I was at the top of my game! I was fortunate to have excelled in all things professionally and being a bit of a "Type A" personality I expected excellence of myself.

February 1, 2004 was the worst night of my life. It was the day that rocked my somewhat secure world. It was like a California earthquake of major proportions including aftershocks. I received a two o'clock in the morning phone call from a "friend" of my then 19 year old son, Matthew, telling me he had been arrested for drug possession. I'm not talking marijuana here! It was speed! I was blindsided. Thus began a journey I never dreamed I'd take. After all, my husband and I did all the "right things" for our kids. I was in shock and as soon as we bailed Matt out of jail we took him kicking and screaming to a chemical dependency program that we were familiar with.

Following this futile appointment were Matt essentially refused treatment, I headed to a local book store to find a resource like "drugs for dummy parents" or anything that could answer the thousands of questions bombarding my brain. To my dismay, there was nothing that met my needs at that time. It took many months and a lot of searching to find some resources to guide me in my quest for understanding. This set into motion my web based search over several months for the information I was starving for. I did eventually find the scientific information I was looking for but, what was missing was the personal testimony of other parents that lived the same nightmare and came out the other side.

Ultimately I found a government web site, National Institute on Drug Abuse (NIDA) that gave me all the facts about teens and drugs, but what I really wanted was something to reassure me that this happens to good families and there is hope for recovery and that there are many resources available to you and how to find them. This book intends to do just that. So, if you have started a journey of your own, I hope this will give you a frame of reference and some reassurance that you are not alone. Remember that above all there is hope

Well, when confronted by Matthew's arrest and subsequent discovery that he is also affected by bipolar disorder I no longer felt that I was an excellent parent. I could not believe that I had missed the fact that Matt was "not normal." I felt I was a failure. After all I was a highly educated health care professional with 30 years of experience. I was an excellent diagnostician and could usually sense when patients were deeply troubled. The reality is that I as a parent wanted to believe the best about my son so my vision of him was cloudy. He was a big kid with a big heart and a big drug habit. I was devastated.

Is this an unusual occurrence in our current society? I think not. Sadly today many parents are confronted with the reality that their teen is a substance abuser. The big question as a parent is where do you turn for accurate information? The problem was especially perplexing for me, having been in practice as a nurse practitioner for over 35 years. How could I as a knowledgeable health care provider have missed the signs in my own child?

About a year later when the dust settled so to speak, I decided to write about drugs and teenagers using Matt's story, and now this has evolved into my story of recovery. I believe the crisis of teenage drug abuse is a common occurrence in today's world and parents need to hear a story of hope and success

It has been more than 8 years since that fateful night and Matt is doing well but this is not the end of his story Although we are told that in some respects he has beat the odds, this will be a life long struggle for Matt and those who love him. We discovered that along with Matt's clinical diagnosis of substance abuse was a dual diagnosis of bipolar disorder. Quite often, teens that use drugs have a coexisting mental health diagnosis like depression, ADD, or bipolar disorder. Treating the mental illness is the first step in treating the substance abuse.

Matt celebrated his eighth year anniversary of being "clean" on November 4, 2012. His bipolar disorder is stable, but he continues to struggle with the symptoms of this disorder. God has blessed us with a good outcome thus far. But nothing is certain. Recovery is a fragile gift. Relapse could happen at any time which ultimately leaves an undertone feeling of unrest. But I have learned to deal with it. Some days have been better than others. So, one of my new realizations is that every day might not be good, but there is something good in every day. It is my hope that you begin to find more and more good in your days.

This book is divided into several sections. The first is Matt's story. Followed by all you as a parent "never really wanted" to know or experience about drugs. Most chapters begin with a quote from Matt. The artwork comes from Matt during the dark times. Yes, we all had dark times in the early days of his recovery. Hard work and many prayers are what pulled us through. It's not so dark anymore but as a parent who wants the best for her now adult child, I still worry. The final chapter is a list of on line resources that may be helpful in your quest for knowledge and understanding. Knowledge is power. I pray that these pages will increase your knowledge about drugs and teens. I hope that you will find the power to work through your current situation and help your child (and yourself) get healthy.

CHAPTER ONE
Matthew's Story

"To every beginning there comes an end, but what if the end
is truly the beginning and beginnings have no end?"

- Matt

February 1, 2004 2 o'clock A.M.

"Is this Matt's mom?"

"Yes."

"This is Andrew. I hate to be the one to tell you this but Matt just got arrested".

"For what?"

"Possession."

"What did he have?"

"Speed."

"Was he the only one who got arrested?"

"Yes."

"Why wasn't any one else arrested?"

"No one else had drugs."

"Is this something new for Matt?"

"Yes, pretty new."

"I gotta go."

THIRTY MINUTES LATER

I called the police department searching for Matt's whereabouts when I had finally collected myself.

Police department

"I just received a call that my son was arrested and I am trying to find out where he is and what to do."

"What's his name?"

"Matthew Gilchrist."

"No, I don't find anything yet. Call back in an hour or so."

SECOND CALL ONE HOUR LATER

My anxiety had risen considerably….

Police department

"I'm trying to locate my son. He was arrested 2 hours ago".

"His name?"

"Matthew Gilchrist, he was arrested near 3rd and Broadway."

"Oh yeah, we just rounded up a bunch of crack cocaine users."

"That's right... c r a c k   c o c a i n e... your son was using c r a c k   c o c a i n e!"

"What should I do?"

"Come in, in the morning with bail and get a public defender."

Needless to say this was not reassuring and I felt sicker than before. A very long hour passed before Matt called.

ANOTHER HOUR PASSES

"Hi mom, did Andrew call you?"

"Yes."

"Please come and get me."

"Is it scary there?"

"Yeah, kind of, just get me soon please."

I laid awake for what was left of the early morning hours. No sleep, no crying, just shock and FEAR! Fear of what was to come. Fear of the unknown. Fear for Matt's safety. Fear for Matt's life. Hopelessness, helplessness, and complete and utter feelings of numbness haunted me.

I was totally unprepared for that first phone call and the visceral reaction that followed. We have all seen the movie version of someone getting bad news who faints dead away. This sounds like an overreaction, right? It was not too far off the real thing for me. I felt dizzy, thought I was going to pass out, got nauseated and felt my blood pressure rise. Then fear and worry kicked in. My first thought was to leave him there to teach him a lesson but after a very early morning phone call to a friend who is an attorney, we were immediately referred to his colleague, who specialized in criminal defense, and we were instructed to get him out as soon as possible since it was Friday and he would be sent to County Jail for the weekend.

We were told that this was a place we definitely did not want our 19 year old son to be sent. We started our day at the office of a local bail bondsman across the street from the court house and police department. I felt fear, anxiety, anger, and humiliation. We were required to pay one thousand dollars to secure the bail bond, and the threat was that if Matt disappeared we would be responsible for $10,000 dollars! We had no idea if Matt would disappear once we bailed him out. Once we had the necessary paperwork, we went to the jail and Matt was released from a side door. His appearance was frightening to me. He looked like a homeless person. The reality was that he was a strung out, disheveled junkie/tweaker/teenager.

Ironically, I had a gut feeling that night as Matt met his friends earlier in the evening on the street in front of our house that something was different. There were kids I had never seen before dressed strangely (goth attire) More importantly I had a feeling that something was off. This prompted me to stay up semi-sleeping on the couch until that horrible phone call came in that night.

Matt has always been a sensitive kid. This has made him very special. His gentle nature makes him great with younger kids, and he has a very tender spot in his heart for his elderly grandmother. From 8th grade on the girls loved him. He is a good listener and as early as age 14 kids were drawn to him to talk about their problems. One of the remarkable statements he made about girls at this age was that "there is more to girls than how they look." He is also incredibly talented artistically. Each year of high school gave him new opportunities to enter art contests and each year Matt would win some kind of art award. To put his talent into perspective, a piece of art he created senior year of high school won a local contest and was displayed in Washington DC at the Capital building for several months.

How did this happen? Matt told me many times when I confronted him about his unusual behavior, before this night that he was not doing drugs. His depression seemed to have worsened of late. But, he reassured me he was not using. I realized now that I wanted desperately to believe this. His behavior leading up to this night should have set off major alarms. His cleanliness slipped, his hair and beard were wild, he reeked of smoke, didn't smell particularly good in general, he often burned incense in his room and I wasn't too crazy about his current friends. Unfortunately, the distracter to recognizing his problem was Matt's 3 years of depression that hit in high school at the age of 16.

Sadly, Matt was often the target of bullying during elementary school. Even though he was larger than most of his peers, they seemed to know that he would not react physically to their torments. Sometimes he was in the perceived in-crowd and sometimes not. Matt, with his sensitive and gentle nature, internalized his feelings. There are times now when I wish we would have allowed him to "deck the kids" who tormented him but our belief and mantra was "You need to solve problems with words not fists." We taught Matt it was important to be kind and considerate of others feelings.

Only in recent years has bullying become more widely recognized. It is no longer regarded as a minor childhood trauma left to kids to work out on their own. National news reports of kids committing suicide after being unable to cope with relentless bullying make this a painful reality. A 2010 study by the Josephson Institute of Ethics indicate that half of 43,321 students surveyed in public and private schools report they had bullied someone in the past year. Forty seven percent said that they were bullied in some manner causing serious upset.

Matt later told me that he always felt different from middle school on. But he also thought that it must just be how kids feel during adolescence. He couldn't figure out how to express this. He said he had mood swings that got progressively worse as he got older. That is when he turned to self medication. He thought drugs would calm the unrest and chaos in his head.

During the early signs of Matt's depression, I decided that his room needed cleaning and I was going to be the one to do it. If you are a mom, you probably understand the occasional need to clean your kid's room. Well something set off a warning and for some reason I looked beyond the surface chaos and found a pack of cigarettes, under which were remnants of marijuana! When confronted, Matt admitted his use of cigarettes and marijuana was to take the edge off his anxiety which was the result of being the target of sexual harassment and bullying at the hands of his fellow team mates at school. It seemed that someone had started a rumor that Matt was gay!

Matt recalls walking to class and being followed by kids who would call him derogatory, gay names. He tells a story about being on the pool deck before practice and two of the older guys got his wallet and played catch with it throwing it over his head. Unfortunately he did not get the support he needed from his coach.

I met with Matt's school counselor who identified what was happening to Matt as sexual harassment and she told me that she wanted to report it to the school vice principal. We were hesitant at first worrying that he would now labeled the "gay snitch" but decided we would go with her recommendation in an effort to reduce Matt's stress. To this day we feel the situation was handled badly by school officials. Matt walked away a victim, leaving a sport he loved, while those who tormented him continued playing the sport and suffering no consequences. We did not know at the time we could have taken a different approach involving law enforcement because sexual harassment is considered a crime on a school campus and the bullies could have been cited and would have had to appear in civil court with their parents.

Matt entered therapy, was given antidepressants, and seemed to be making progress. "SEEMED TO" turned out to be wishful thinking on my part. He continued with high school, tried to convince us that he was affected by ADD (probably figuring he could get Adderall) and continued to dabble in drugs. By the time he graduated from high school, he had a full blown speed habit, and actually went through graduation high.

Through all of this Matt continued to hold down a job in a mobile skate park where he unfortunately was exposed to people in the community where he worked who introduced him to other drugs: speed and heroin. Realistically, I know that he could have met these people in any setting in his life. You can't control who your teen comes in contact with during his hours away from home

Matt had always enjoyed looking different, so his thrift shop (vintage) attire and full beard and crazy blonde "fro" seemed to be more of an attempt to be unique than a warning sign. What I did not notice was that his layered "Seattle grunge" look as he called it was hiding a significant weight loss. During the end of his senior year of high school we did notice what appeared to be a healthy weight loss and Matt told us it was due to giving up fast food. He had always been a bit overweight and now looked "buff." What we didn't know was that he had given up eating all together. The anorexia caused by the use of speed had made him seem to be of normal weight. Through all of this turmoil and dysfunction he managed to hold down a job, finish high school (barely) and seemed like a fairly normal but rebellious kid. He masterfully manipulated his parents, and therapist into thinking that this was normal teenage angst. Matt tells me he would intentionally withhold significant information from his therapist. Once he graduated from high school he stopped therapy stating that the stress of school was gone and he felt he could deal with things on his own.

The harassment that Matt experienced in high school resulted in his departure from the school sport that he loved. Matt was also moved from his gifted education program to "regular school." Matt's circle of friends changed dramatically. Matt had a strong connection to two friends. Tim and Reana lived with her mom (also a speed user) and Matt spent many hours with them. Matt conned me into believing that they were supporting each other in their efforts to get clean. In essence they were supporting each others drug habit. Tim got kicked out of that living arrangement and actually lived with us for a while on a ratty old couch that they moved into Matt's room.

I thought it was my duty to reach out and save a kid from street life until he could make other arrangements. This turned out to be a bad move. After 2 weeks we asked him to leave. During the period of time we took away Matt's car privileges, I was in rare form practicing enabling, I would drive him to their house (my rationale was I would not have to worry he would get picked up by the police while riding his skate board late at night across town). I bought him cigarettes for a while because he said that they would keep him from having serious cravings to his drug of choice. This was of course fabricated "logic" that I fell for wanting desperately to prevent more serious events from happening.

During this time Matt had a "garage band" that practiced at our place. They were all users as well and good at hiding signs of use. In retrospect I realized all of the boys had some kind of psychiatric disorder. One had actually been "lost in the juvenile justice system for 3 years and the other affected by ADD. Also looking back I am amazed that we did not have issues with neighbors or police.

Matt registered for and attended community college for just short of one semester when he seemed to have a nervous breakdown and withdrew from school. He calls this his psychotic break. I remember the night vividly. Matt had an art project due the next day and stayed up late. In the morning when I checked with him before I left for work, shockingly, he was covered from head to toe with charcoal which he had been using for his project. He looked like a cave man!

After this incident, Matt stopped attending college but continued working. He refused to go back to his counselor insisting that he was not severely depressed. But we kept working on him hoping he would see the need. In retrospect, I probably wanted to believe that depression and 18 year old rebellion was at the root of his behavior. I ignored my gut feelings, blinding myself to signs of other problems.

Speed was only the tip of the iceberg. During the early stages of Matt's recovery he began to share his story of entry level substance abuse, beer, cigarettes, alcohol moving on to speed, mushrooms and ultimately heroin.

It still baffles me that my son is a drug addict. As parents we had always tried to do the right things for our kids. We gave them lots of love and affection, and worked on their self esteem. They were involved in school activities, sports, scouts, and church activities. We took many family vacations. Some of the most memorable were to Mammoth Mountain in California. We have a very close extended family with grandparents, aunts and uncles near by. Matt got the usual no drugs, no alcohol, no smoking messages as he grew up. We participated in Dare to Say No and Red Ribbon activities at school. He posted anti drug stickers in his room. He won a Los Angeles County award for an anti-smoking art project he submitted to a contest. (Ironically, he was smoking and using at the time.)

Of course as parents, my husband and I wondered what we did wrong. The answer is nothing. Kids have free will and make their own choices. Teens can make bad choices and do stupid things regardless of where you attempt to lead them. The adolescent brain is neither experienced nor developed enough to ensure that every choice they make is a good one.

There's no going back, only forward. Every day I hope and pray that Matt remains clean. That underlying fear of relapse is always there and I worry. I have no control over the choices he makes. It is a difficult, but important lesson we must learn as parents that we have no control over the choices our children make in life or in recovery. We can only offer advice and be here to support our children and guide them along the path of healthy living. In the end, their choices are their own.

Matt is now 28 and has made incredible progress. At the age of 19 we had to do a tough love parental intervention to force him into a treatment program for his addiction and coexisting bipolar disorder. Following his four month residential treatment program the court dismissed his drug possession charges so fortunately his record is clean. Matt remains clean and sober, has participated in a dual diagnosis program, attends counseling with a therapist, and sees a psychiatrist and takes medications for his underlying mental health diagnosis. He says he can't imagine using substances (especially speed, but he does have some concerns about heroin because of the feeling it gave him) in the future now that his condition is being treated With that said, he also knows that he will never be free of the possibility of a relapse. My husband and I also know this and it is a frightening reality. Recovery is a fragile gift.

I was reading the local newspaper recently when an obituary of a young man, one year older than Matt caught my eye. By the time I finished reading it I was crying because I know the obituary I was reading could have been my son's. It started out "a big sweet guy passed away. Enduring a life of depression and a long struggle with addiction he fit a lot of life into his 27 years before his accidental death." He was also named Matthew. I am again crying as I write this because I am reminded that this could still happen to my Matt in the future. I can only imagine how his mother felt losing him with the promise of a potential life helping others in his twelve step program. The description of his involvement with sports and his connection to his 86 year old grandpa his success at college paralleled my son's life. His obituary talked about the ravages of addiction and gives the powerful message that addiction is deadly serious and that recovery is a precious gift. Those of us who have passed through this experience must help others.

CHAPTER TWO
Teens and Drug Abuse

I never expected to have such a monumental parenting issue to deal with. Drugs! What mother wants to admit her child is an addict? I sure never dreamed this would be me. Before my nightmare began I thought I had a decent working knowledge about drug abuse. My own personal experience was limited to maybe a little too much alcohol at a party or a "hit" from a marijuana joint in the 70's.

However, in my quest to understand Matt better, I did extensive research and learned more than I ever really wanted to know about drugs. The most significant study about teens and drug use, Monitoring the Future, is done on an annual basis by the University of Michigan and sponsored by the National Institute on Drug Abuse. This is an ongoing study of behavior, attitudes, and values of American secondary school students, college students and young adults. Each year since 1991, a total of approximately 50,000 8th, 10th and 12th grade students are surveyed. In addition, annual follow-up questionnaires are mailed to a sample of each graduating class for a number of years after their initial participation.

The most recent studies were released in 2011 and the overall indication is that use of **any** illicit drug by American teens has risen gradually over the past four years due to increased use of marijuana. However, the use of any illicit drug other than marijuana has been stable for thee years. The recent studies show a continued small decline in the use of amphetamines, Ritalin, methamphetamines, and crystal methamphetamine. Some drugs showed little change. Cocaine, crack cocaine, LSD, hallucinogens other than LSD and heroin remained steady. Abuse of prescription type drugs outside of medical supervision include; sedatives, tranquilizers, oxycotin and vicodin. These continue to be a problem. Cocaine use reached a peak in 1990, declined for a year or two and has remained constant ever since. The prevalence is between 2-5% in grades 8, 10 and 12.

One drug in particular that has gained in popularity is MDMA (ecstasy). An increase in use has shown up in the upper grades. Over the counter cough and cold medicines are also being used by kids to get high. The ingredient dextromethorphen is one active ingredient teens look for. This is found most often in over the counter cough preparations such as Delsym and Robitussin. This seemingly innocuous, over the counter cold remedy can cause stimulant effects, distorted visual perceptions, a sense of disassociation from the body, confusion, hallucinations, and dizziness. It can also have depressive effects.

Parents underestimate their teen's exposure to drugs. Shockingly one quarter of high school students have been offered, given, or sold illicit drugs on school grounds. Alcohol is the most commonly used drug in high school students, with marijuana also a concern. These can be considered gateway drugs. Matt told us it was "way easier to get drugs while in high school on the campus than after graduation."

Some highlights follow:
- **Cigarette smoking declined in the lower grades (eighth and tenth)**
- **Use of stimulants declined among 10th graders including crystal methamphetamine**
- **Alcohol use in 10th graders decreased**
- **Marijuana use has been rising for the past three years**
- **Daily marijuana use increased in all three grades**
- **One in fifteen high school seniors today are smoking pot daily or nearly daily. This is the highest rate since 1981**
- **Vicodin continues to be abused at high levels**
- **The use of over the counter cough preparations dropped in all ages**
- **Energy drinks are used by heavily by teens, mostly in younger teens**

"Monitoring the Future" is a self reported survey and may actually under represent drug use due to drop outs and truants not being represented. In 2011 when asked about use of substances during the past twelve months high school seniors reported the following:

Percentage of students who admitted to using:
- **Marijuana 36.4%**
- **Spice 11.4%**
- **Ecstasy 5.3%**
- **Hallucinogens 5.2%**
- **Cocaine 2.9%**

Another excellent source of information is The National Center of Addiction and Substance Abuse at Columbia University (CASA). The annual 2011 study results indicate some concerning trends:

- **60% of teens attend schools where drugs are used, kept, or sold at school**
- **42% of 12-17 year olds know at least one friend who uses substances**
- **Visiting social networking sites puts teens at increased risk for substance abuse**

Teens that use social network sites are:
- **5 times more likely to use tobacco**
- **3 times more likely to use alcohol**
- **2 times more likely to use marijuana**

There is a relationship between the site images and increased use of substances by teens who view these images. The old adage, "one picture is worth 1000 words" seems to hold true. When quizzed, parents state that they do not believe that social networking sites would make their child more likely to use substances

Sometimes we as parents need a wakeup call. Mine literally came as a phone call at two A.M. It would seem that on a certain level that there is a problem but we don't want to accept it or know the true extent because it is really scary and makes us feel as though we've failed as parents. Then feelings of frustration and guilt come into play so we investigate to a certain degree but convince ourselves it's not really a huge problem and end up ignoring significant signs and symptoms in our kids. There are many signs that may indicate your kid is using. Sometimes they are subtle like the use of incense, and other times they're as blatant as finding a used pipe. Finding drug paraphernalia in your teen's room is a gut wrenching experience as it was for me, but generally there are other signs that your kid is using.

I was fortunate to have good friends and professional associates whom I could talk with, but there were still details I did not share. Shame and guilt certainly do take over. These were feelings that I could only share with my closest friends. It's okay to have these feelings, but important to realize that this is not your fault and there's no reason to be embarrassed. You are not the only parent in the history of the world to be affected by this horrible disease.

I remember at one time thinking how lucky we were that Matt and his friends liked to hang out in our garage with their garage band. Little did I know that those evenings included drug use. I thought at that time, "well he is home and I know he is not running around get into trouble." Sure…but he and his friends got real good at predicting when I would come out to do laundry or bring them food and confidently used their drugs in my garage. Boy did I feel dumb later! Studies show that parents who are at home during their teens parties have no clue that the teens are using in their own home.

CHAPTER THREE
Detoxification "Detox"

HELL

"Heaven smiles above me, but hell welcomes me in."
~ Matt

When we first bailed Matt out of jail he insisted we stop at the house of the kid he was with the night was arrested. He wanted to pick up his "things." Little did we know that we were actually stopping to pick up his drugs. Lesson one: ADDICTS

LIE. We then took him, kicking and screaming, to a chemical dependency recovery program. (CDRP) He left, declining admission for inpatient "detox" feeling he could do it his own. Lesson two: No matter what you want, the addict has to want treatment. Matt says now with clarity of mind that he regrets his decision to refuse inpatient detoxification.

Lesson three: Once your teen is over 18, legally they can refuse treatment. (Even though they still depend upon you for a home, car, or other forms of support.) Your desire to have them admitted to a treatment facility holds no legal ground.

If your teen is eighteen or older, and is out of control, there are ways to get legal jurisdiction over them. It requires getting a lawyer and going to court. If you do choose to allow your drug abusing teen to live at home during rehab it is very important to set limits and stick to them. This means a serious talk about what you will and will not permit in your home. Drawing up a contract including rules to be followed at home, stipulations for work or school attendance, room and board charges and accountability if they break the contract is extremely important. Follow through is essential. In our case, we tolerated behavior we shouldn't have primarily based on my fear of grave consequences to Matthew if we forced him to leave our home. Enabling an addict is detrimental to their recovery and your sanity! In the case of a minor, my bias and advice is to find a live in treatment program immediately. An addict needs to be removed from the friends, situations, and the environment that enable him to use.

In Matt's case we went to three separate locations trying to find a program he "felt good about". He agreed to an outpatient detox program at the second facility but unfortunately was being treated by a health care provider that was probably just as crazy as he was at the time. In this program we went daily to the facility to check in and pick up medications to assist with the detox process. During this week I stayed home from work because he needed transportation to the office. I feared leaving him at home alone knowing that anything could happen since now I clearly knew he was an addict. This was not a pleasant way to use my saved vacation hours, but fortunately I could take the time off without work consequences.

Matt slept 20 out of 24 hours a day. When he came out of his room for food he was angry, agitated, and down right scary. On one occasion we had words at the front door and in his angry, drugged state he proceeded to kick a hole through the wall. My daughter and I witnessed this and were scared. All I could do was hope and pray that he would not act out physically, and trust that eventually his innate gentle nature would prevail. Sadly my husband was out of town on business so I did not have another adult supporting me at home. I did have many supportive friends just a phone call away. I felt that I had to be "strong" for my daughter's sake. Somehow we made it through that time without major incident. Soon after this horrific time, miraculously Matt established a relationship with a psychiatrist at the third program we visited who was instrumental in starting him on the right path to recovery. Even though he continued to resist the advice to be hospitalized somehow he participated marginally in a recovery program that kept him at home, off the street, and out of jail.

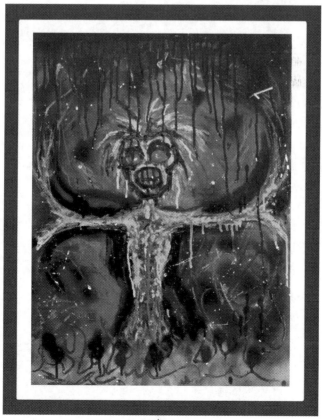

DETOX

When teens abruptly stop using drugs there are many behaviors you might see. Anxiety, depression, restlessness, sleeplessness, anger, paranoia, and aggressiveness are common. I strongly advise you to get professional help for your teen during this time. While Matt was going through detox, without professional help, I was afraid of what he might do, but deep down I wanted desperately to believe he would not become violent.

Medications may help suppress withdrawal symptoms due to detoxification. But, keep in mind medical help with withdrawal is not by itself treatment for drug addiction—just the first step. Medications are used to help restore normal brain functioning and prevent immediate relapse and craving during early treatment. There are medications to assist with heroin, morphine, and nicotine withdrawal but absolutely nothing for speed. According to the NIDA, currently drugs are being developed for use with cocaine, speed and marijuana withdrawal.

PART 2 - HOW COULD THIS HAVE HAPPENED to US?

CHAPTER FOUR
Understanding Drug Abuse

"Insanity---a summer when it's wintertime."
~ Matt

People's general understanding of drug abuse has changed dramatically in the past 10 years. In the past, it was believed addicts were criminals or morally weak people who could stop if they just changed their behavior. Drug abuse was viewed as a social problem. Today, drug addiction is recognized as a chronic but treatable disease. It crosses all segments of the population, young and old rich and poor. It is chronic and relapsing, is common, but it is a treatable condition. Understanding drug abuse helps us understand how to prevent it in the first place. The National Institute on Drug Abuse prevention research has shown that "comprehensive prevention programs that involve the family, schools, communities and the media are effective in reducing drug abuse." All these agencies must send the message that it's better to avoid using than to rehabilitate afterward.

How the brain works

To understand how addiction happens we need to understand how the brain works and how it processes messages from chemical messengers called neurotransmitters. The brain has different centers or systems that process different types of information. The brainstem at the base of the brain is the primitive structure that is responsible for heart activity, breathing and sleeping. These are autonomic activities that we don't consciously think about. The brain is separated into lobes that receive sensory information and produce responses. Specifically, the occipital lobe receives information from sensory organs. In contrast, the cortex is the thinking part of the brain. Deep inside this cortex is the limbic system which is responsible for survival. It creates memories for things that keep you alive like eating food, drinking fluids and seeking companionship. The cerebellum remembers things that we learn once in our lifetime like balance, walking, and other motor movements that require coordination.

All these components work together to process information. Brain cells called neurons receive and process information. This message is an electrical impulse. Once it reaches it's destination it causes a release of a chemical called a neurotransmitter. This is the key to understanding drug abuse. Drugs affect the release or block the release of neurotransmitters, so there is an unnatural chain reaction of electrical charges in the brain when one uses drugs. Drugs like nicotine, cocaine, speed, and marijuana affect the brain's "survival system" (limbic system). Mood altering drugs influence neurotransmitters which are responsible for communication between brain cells. They change how often and how strong the messages are sent.

Neurotransmitters (chemical messengers)

There are two neurotransmitters that are important when trying to understanding addiction: dopamine and serotonin. These messengers affect the response to life events, moods, social behavior, and motivate us to bring peace to our life. When the balance is normal the messengers work together. Dopamine has central roles in the body. It focuses our attention, and activates behavior. This increases our level of arousal. Our awareness is heightened and senses are alert. Dopamine drives the motor system. In an emergency, dopamine is converted to adrenalin. Dopamine has a key role in addictive behavior. Too much dopamine causes one to be very focused, too little causes depression, foggy thinking or inability to block extra signals. Serotonin on the other hand makes us feel safe and satisfied. It acts as an anti-impulsive agent. When serotonin is released we are calm, content, and feel our energy get smoother.

Serotonin keeps dopamine's actions in check. Too little serotonin makes us irritable. Signs are anger, aggressive behavior, and impulsivity. Thoughts may be obsessive and the brain gets overloaded and can't process information. Too much serotonin makes it hard to remember things. Without the proper balance of the neurotransmitters, people are driven to seek any solution to end pain or uncomfortable and uneasy feelings. Chronic stress lowers natural levels of serotonin. "The drive to stop this longing becomes critical and clear. This is craving"

CHAPTER FIVE

Craving

"You crawl across the floor on your hands and knees in search of Something unknown, I pull you up and give you a false sense of hope. Bow down before me for I am the creator as well as the destroyer And I'm coming out."

~ Matt

Craving is uncomfortable. Craving causes stress. We become motivated to find behaviors that restore feelings of contentment. Fear, pain, or low self esteem can cause the brain to try to adapt to these unwanted states, which sets the stage for addiction. Stress can lead to substance abuse particularly if that stress is based in a feeling of not belonging or not feeling safe. In addition, an individual's hormones, life experiences and messages the brain receives influence subsequent responses. This can lower natural neurotransmitter levels, most specifically serotonin resulting in unwanted feelings.

Craving is an extreme biological response. Desire, want, and need are normal, but craving moves beyond this. Craving involves an element of obsession. This is highly affected by our mental state and physical setting. What then produces addictive responses and behaviors? Substances that raise dopamine levels in the limbic system cause conditioned learning responses that lead to reactions. So the brain becomes sensitized to exposure to drugs and produces addictive behavior in the form of compulsive drug seeking and taking.

Craving becomes a conditioned stimulus. This is much like Pavlov and the salivating dogs. For instance, when we see, smell or think about food, dopamine is released in our brain. We eat and our craving is satisfied. However, in an addict battling drugs, the sight, a sound, or thought of a drug leads to ingestion or use.

This increases dopamine and becomes a conditioned learning response.

Craving brains are produced by genetics, hormones, and the environment. The craving response is directed to anything that unconditionally releases dopamine and that can be associated with anticipation of the object or activities. Craving is influenced by stimuli--for instance, alcoholics respond to a glass with ice cubes and junkies a syringe. The mental state and physical setting are important. It is critical to know what these stimuli are in order to keep them away.

Cravings are part of the human condition. For example, on a much smaller scale, I crave chocolate on occasion. Research suggests some people have better "stop systems" or better brakes. It is important in recovery to remember that craving does not mean that an addict is unmotivated or doomed to relapse. Learning what triggers cravings is an important part of recovery. Sometimes craving can't be avoided and there are some coping strategies that you might help your teen to cultivate.

- **Distraction: getting involved in distracting activities such as reading, hobbies, going to the movies, or exercise**
- **Talk it through: reach out to a trusted friend, family member, or sponsor**
- **Challenge and change thoughts. Craving brings up "good" memories of drug use. Redirect thoughts to the bad effects of drug use**
- **Harmless temporary solutions like candy, trail mix, or gum**
- **Post lists of reasons to quit**

CHAPTER SIX
Addiction
Addiction Canges The Will

"A Day of Gray"

"Up all night, another restless slumber.
Numbness takes over, I'm in fright.
How can one let their self get to this point?
Colorless visions as the new morning arrives.
Everything is nothing but shades of gray in a tweaker's eyes."
~ Matt

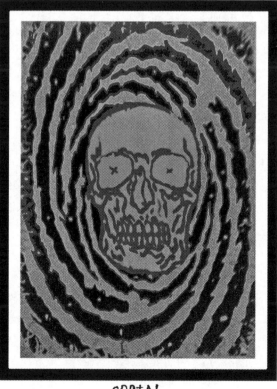

SPRIAL

What is addiction? The term comes from a Latin word which means to "give oneself up" or to give oneself over to another power. According to the National Institute on Drug Abuse and Addiction, addiction is defined as a "chronic, relapsing brain disease that is characterized by compulsive drug seeking and use, despite harmful consequences." It is considered a brain disease because drugs change the brain, its structure, and how it works. Another way to look at addiction is a compulsive need for and use of a habit-forming substance characterized by tolerance and by well defined physiological symptoms upon withdrawal. It is a persistent and compulsive use of a substance known by the user to be harmful. Addiction is a disease that affects the brain, by altering chemical levels resulting in behaviors.

Addiction is a gradual process and there is a huge variation in the way individuals become addicted. The intensity of addiction is related to the substance or activity. Shockingly, it has been said that everyone is a potential addict. So why are some people hugely affected and others not? Hardiman's book **ADDICTION** identifies three key elements that can explain why people become addicted. The first is the nature of the substance. For instance, cigarette smoking is highly addictive. This seems to be the best example and easily understood. Nicotine enters and leaves the body quickly. The smoker quickly becomes hooked on the stimulating effect. Once nicotine clears the body, usually in 30 minutes or so, the smoker craves more. With nicotine, there is a very mild physical craving, akin to caffeine and smokers' brains are trained to the habits that are pleasurable they associate with smoking. Contrary to both popular belief and some professionals and recovery specialist, the smoker has a choice. (brain wise) Where as the alcoholic and addicts after a certain amount of time drinking and using, has little choice regarding quitting. Addicts are responding to very strong driving forces, mainly in their brain chemistry.

Another element is the motivation behind a person's need to change their mood artificially. Addicts begin using to produce pleasure, or escape from reality. Once they realize this can be achieved with the use of certain drugs, they desire to repeat the experience. They may want to continue with feelings of elation, excitement, or simply to relieve anxiety or emotional distress. Other substances create a feeling of power or confidence or connection and unity.

The last key element is the individual's physical vulnerability to a substance. Hardiman states that some people seem to be more prone to drug addiction than others. This has to do with several theories. Genetics contributes to addiction, as does environment. According to the National Institute on Drug Abuse, scientists estimate that genetics account for 40-60% of a persons vulnerability to drug abuse and that adolescents and people with mental disorders are at greater risk when compared to the general population. In addition, how the brain interacts with chemicals or experiences that alter the brain environment adds to the addictive process.

The following definitions may help you understand how the disease of addiction progresses and the nature of drug abuse. These definitions come from the American Medical Association Counsel on Scientific Affairs Task Force of the Panel on Alcoholism and Drug Abuse 2000. These are in general use in the medical community.

Abuse: use that causes physical, psychological, economic, legal or social harm

Intoxication: changes in the body's physiology as a result of using a substance

Addiction: chronic compulsive use of a substance

Physiologic dependence: emotional craving

Physical dependence: adaptation to drugs causing tolerance and withdrawal

Use: sporadic consumption of drugs or alcohol with no adverse consequences

Adolescence is a time when peers have a huge impact on choices your teen makes. Peer pressure weighs heavily on the choices even if there are no other risk factors. Research indicates that the earlier the introduction to drugs, the more likely it is that it will lead to serious drug abuse. Drugs change how the brain works. The teen brain is still growing (actually until about age of 25) Since adolescence is a time where teens are learning to make good decisions, drug use can prevent meeting important developmental milestones much like an infant learning to walk.

I have been told that a teen can get stuck in the developmental stage they were in when they began to heavily use drugs. I view this as arrested development. For several years after Matt left rehab, although he was in his 20's, his behaviors seemed more like that of a high school teen. Matt's socialization was definitely delayed by this drug use but he is making drastic improvements. I believe he will get to where he is supposed to be in his own time.

Addictive theory dates back 200 years and was built on the premise that it is a loss of control and the only remedy is abstinence. Early attempts to understand the addictive personality looked at an addict as an emotionally immature and easily frustrated individual who had little or no will power and was generally irresponsible. Today we know that you cannot stereotype addicts because they cross all sections of society. One thing is certain, according to Hardiman "ADDICTS FALL IN LOVE WITH THEIR DRUG OF CHOICE AND BUILD A STRONG EMOTIONAL ATTACHMENT TO IT" Their addiction hides personal difficulties and keeps them from maturing and leading emotionally healthy lives. The addict's life becomes chaotic and unmanageable. They are constantly looking for highs and fixes at the expense of all else.

Addicts develop elaborate and distorted ways of seeing things, which allows them to tolerate anxiety and pain and ignore the effects of addiction. The drug of choice is determined by the experience the user seeks. Weed creates a mellow mood. Speed makes people highly alert. Mushrooms distort reality. The "gotta have it" (craving) drives the addict. They spend more and more time and energy to obtain and use their drug of choice. An addict's primary purpose in life is to seek and use drugs. Matthew said that the pursuit of the drug was just about as addictive as using it. Searching out the supplier or driving all over town to find the next fix became part of the pleasure.

Sadly, since drug abuse is a chronic (life long) disease, relapse is common. The National Institute on Drug Abuse states that relapse is not only possible, but likely. Treatment of any chronic disease like diabetes or asthma involves changing behaviors. Relapse does not mean failure but indicates a need to retune treatment methods or try something new.

How do you change behaviors? In Matt's case it involved getting rid of all his drug friends, moving him to a new isolated location so that they could not have contact with him and beginning a plan to change his mind set. All of that was achieved by forcing him into a rehabilitation facility. As time wore on the bad friends stopped calling and upon his return home only on rare occasions would a call come in to the house. Generally I intercepted them and did not share that information for days or weeks later. Kids are so fragile in recovery. The protective "mother bear" came out in me more than once. This was very difficult for Matt who had always been a very social kid. He felt isolated and "friends" in therapy were supportive but did not provide the close connection he craved. Sadly, using drugs in some instances gives a feeling of connectedness or community.

One distressing call did come in though. It was from Reana (mentioned in a previous chapter) who along with her boyfriend lived at her mother's house. (The mother was also a speed addict.) She called one night trying to find out where Matt was living. She was persistent and I was not sure of her motivation. Did she want to find him and reconnect? As the call progressed, it turned out the boyfriend was gone and she really wanted to get clean but did not know where to start. After determining that she was not suicidal, we talked about treatment options. I advised the emergency room as a starting place if she was in bad shape. Additionally, I suggested she see her family doctor or call her health plan for resources available to her. I stressed the availability of Narcotics anonymous (NA) and hoped for the best. Matt recently heard she was clean and in college.

DEATH

PART 3 -
WELCOME TO CHAOS

CHAPTER SEVEN
Could My Kid Be Using?

"Would it be so hard to pretend you are happy?"
~ Matt

If only there was an easy explanation to why some teens get hopelessly addicted or even try drugs, families and society in general could make strides in prevention. Teen drug use is very complex. Some kids use out of boredom, curiosity, rebellion or for peer acceptance. Adolescence is a developmental time marked by experimentation. Most parents hope that their teen will not experiment with drugs and some fortunately get their wish. However, some of us live this other nightmare. Often depression, attention deficit disorder, bipolar disorder, eating disorders, post traumatic stress, fetal alcohol syndrome, schizophrenia, and social anxiety can be part of the drug use equation. I n a misguided attempt at self medication the result is often addiction. Mental heath problems often overlap with substance abuse. Teen substance abuse can progress rapidly from experimentation and occasional use to dependency and abuse. Teens use substances for many of the same reasons that adults do. The need to relax, to feel good, and to feel more social is not unique to adolescents.

Parents underestimate their teen's exposure to drugs. Shockingly one quarter of high school students have been offered, given, or sold illicit drugs on school grounds. Alcohol is the most commonly used drug in high school students, with marijuana also a concern. These can be considered gateway drugs. Matt told us it was "way easier to get drugs while in high school on the campus than after graduation."

Sometimes we as parents need a wake up call. Mine literally came as a phone call at two A.M. It would seem that on a certain level that there is a problem but we don't want to accept it or know the true extent because it is really scary and makes us feel as though we've failed as parents. Then feelings of frustration and guilt come into play so we investigate to a certain degree but convince ourselves it's not really a huge problem and end up ignoring significant signs and symptoms in our kids. There are many signs that may indicate your kid is using. Sometimes they are subtle like the use of incense, and other times they're as blatant as finding a used pipe. Finding drug paraphernalia in your teen's room is a gut wrenching experience; it was for me, but generally there are other signs that your kid is using.

I must have found and destroyed over 20 different types of bongs, pipes and other paraphernalia once we discovered Matt was a user. I would put them in a brown bag and angrily smash them with a hammer which would feel good for a moment, but the overwhelming feelings of fear and sadness remained. Everything I found was quickly replaced and hidden in new hiding spots. In retrospect I realize that this became an unhealthy game of "search and destroy" where I made frequent checks of his room. This served no purpose other than to make me crazy. I was fortunate to have good friends and professional associates that I could talk to, but there were still details I did not share with them. I was also dealing with feelings of shame and guilt that I could only share with my closest friends. It's okay to have these feelings, but important to realize that this is not your fault and there's no reason to be embarrassed. You are not the only parent in the history of the world to be affected by this horrible disease.

Here is a quick reference guide to signs your kid may be using:
- **Mood swings**
- **Lying (often to themselves)**
- **Unexplained absence from home**
- **Physically recurrent illness**
- **Making up stories to get money**
- **Anger**
- **Poor personal hygiene**
- **Drastic change in appearance**

- **Constant picking**
- **Sores on legs and arms**
- **Foil balls on floor of room**
- **Pens taken apart**
- **Straws scattered around the bedroom**
- **Black q-tips**
- **Incense use**
- **Sudden use of cologne, eye drops, Nyquil**
- **Slurred speech**
- **Weight loss**
- **Layered clothing**
- **Bottles of Niacin tablets**
- **Wears black a lot**
- **Gadgets in room (little things built with batteries, wires, duct tape)**

Matt exhibited at least half of these behaviors. However, I did not put the pieces of the puzzle together. Taken individually they might be easy to overlook. Plus my naiveté made me miss things. I remember often picking up small pieces of foil balled up in his room. They did not mean anything to me at the time but I now know that this is how they "cook drugs." Deconstructed disposable pens serve as pipes for smoking drugs or snorting powdered drugs like cocaine. Straws are also used for this. Incense hides body odor when rubbed on clothing and when burned camouflages drug odors. Had I been more observant I would have seen that Matt had scabs on his legs from "picking." These sores are signs of an obsessive behavior and can be mistaken for flea bites that have been scratched.

Pronounced changes in your teen's behavior could mean drug use. It could also mean mental illness, situational stress, the result of physical abuse, or harassment. One big change with kids who use is all of a sudden they have a new set of friends. This kind of change is done at the expense of kids that they once had a lot in common with. Sports, dance, or work friends fall by the way side. Matt told me he got to a point where he believed his "friends did not understand him." He started hanging out with a different crowd and unknown to me started skipping class. He felt the new friends understood him and didn't judge him. He says at this point he switched from being a "cool, happy-go-lucky kid to an outcast, misfit, and angry at the world." He lacked motivation in school and since his new friends were going to continuation school, Matt was pushing us to let him finish school this way. We stood our ground and did not permit it. Fortunately with the help of 2 wonderful teachers, extra tutoring and our persistence Matt raised his D's and F to C's and B's in 8 weeks and graduated with a high school diploma. Teens who are abusing substances, may fall behind in their school work affecting their grades. Lack of interest in previously loved activities is a really important sign. Apathy often follows as does physical violence, acting out against a sibling or other family member. These are all are signs of trouble.

Violent behavior is a big sign. Mood swings, outbursts, or hostility directed at the family are worrisome. At the height of his disease my son began acting out against his sister. One incident particularly comes to mind. Megan had baked a pumpkin pie totally from scratch and it was cooling in the kitchen. She and I discovered that "someone" had taken a fork to the pie and totally mutilated it. I don't just mean eating it. It was violently destroyed. The fear that Matt would harm someone is ultimately what prompted me to stop enabling him and force him into a live in program.

It was this behavior which served as another wake up call for me. I finally realized that things could get a lot worse and this is what prompted an intervention. Matt was scheduled for a counseling appointment with his therapist. I was able to call the counselor prior to the appointment time to alert him to my concerns and we set up a plan of action. He made arrangements for Matt to be admitted to the mental health facility that night in a holding and detox intermediate unit before being transferred to an isolated Twelve Step Social Model Recovery Center. During the session we gave Matt the message he could no longer live at home with the behaviors he was showing and would either have to be admitted or leave our home. He refused! Defiantly he said he would be leaving our home that night. (More about that night will be explained later)

Verbal abuse directed at parents and friends is particularly concerning. Teens get very secretive when they use substances. Also important to note are evasive answers and outright lies about where they are going, have been or curfew violations. Sound like anyone you know? Oddly, Matt always kept curfew. I gather it was a manipulative move to keep under our radar.

Stealing money or valuables from the house to support their drug habit is also common. Quite often, although I dismissed it as my forgetfulness, I would be missing $20 here or there. Sometimes it would be $40 and that is when I began suspecting. My son was very good at not disturbing the placement of my purse or contents within, but he was stealing. When I finally began to confront him about it he would say he would never stoop that low. (That phrase became a mantra for Matt and I'm not sure who he was trying to convince; me or him.)

He lied and amazingly I believed him! He was always very controlled in his answers to questioning about possible drug use. His verbal responses were calm, controlled, his body language was normal, and he would reassure me that that if he had a problem he would definitely come to us for help. Beware, drug addicts LIE. Reckless behavior is another sign. These are behaviors that put themselves, their friends or family at risk.

Listen to your inner voice. As parents we generally know something is not right on a certain level, but we really don't want to confront it. Admitting this is to admit we have failed. I ask myself very often how I could have missed Matt's drug use. I think we do this because we love our kids and want to believe the best about them. Love your kid! Recognize that something is wrong. ACT ON IT! Confront your worse fear and early intervention could ultimately save your kid's life. You need to stop the progression of the disease.

Talk to your family physician about resources available to you in your heath plan or community. There are organizations like Alcoholics Anonymous (AA), Narcotics Anonymous NA, or Narc-anon you can call 24/7 to find a meeting in your community. It's easy to go on line or to call information for an 800 telephone number and someone will talk to you right then and there. These are self help organizations where addicts or family of addicts support each other. I made many calls for advice and spoke to members who were very knowledgeable about what addicts do because they had been there. These organizations support not only the addict but family members as well. Seek counseling from an addiction specialist. Also read, read, read all you can about addiction. In a later chapter you will find recommended websites and references.

Don't enable your kid to continue behaviors. We are great at making excuses for our teen or preventing them from experiencing the consequences of their actions. I became very skilled at enabling Matt to continue his behaviors long after I should have taken action. This is something I regret. It was also a source of stress between my husband and me. Realize you can not change an addict. Change has to come from their own realization that they are on a downward spiral of destruction. You can change your response to the addict which in turn may stimulate a change in the addict. I now know that my desire to keep things "stable" and protect Matt from consequences (i.e. jail time, overdose or death) enabled him to continue his drug use longer than he should have.

It is easy to slip into feelings of guilt. DON'T BUY INTO IT! We feel somehow responsible and ask how we failed our son or daughter. Maybe we really are bad parents. These thoughts are most probably not true. Remember it is their choice to use, not yours. You did not give them permission to use drugs. It is their bad choice and they will have to experience the painful consequences. Unfortunately you are suffering the fall out from their bad choices as well. As adults we see more clearly the consequences of their drug use and in the case of an arrest, the consequences of having a police record.

Matthew did not understand that being arrested, or convicted of a misdemeanor drug possession, or in his case that a felony (later reduced to a misdemeanor and ultimately dismissed) could have major, negative effects on his adult life. He had no concept that choice of professions, jobs, or even college could be adversely affected. Once out of jail on the night of his arrest he became quite cavalier about his nine hours in jail, finding it more of a "psychological study" of people in jail rather than the life altering experience it was.

Do not keep this a secret. Talk about your situation. You may find support in many unexpected places. In talking to my friends after we discovered Matt's secret I found several of my professional colleagues had had similar experiences with their kids who were now normal adults. Talking about your experience may make others comfortable with sharing their own difficult experiences. Both my husband and I are very open about sharing Matt's experience. Matt completely supports our openness.

Once I was at the makeup counter at a local department store and was talking to the young sales person and she asked if I had kids. I shared with her that my daughter was in college and my son in rehab. She asked me to tell her about Matt and when I went into details she very pointedly looked at me, grabbed my hand and stated that she was a current meth user and didn't know how to start dealing with it. I spent about 20 minutes doing an intervention in the makeup department! We drew up a loose plan of action. She agreed to talk to her parents, go to a NA (narcotics anonymous) meeting within the week. I spoke to her weekly for 3 weeks and she did eventually follow though with her plan, in her own time. The last time we spoke her family was looking for a hospital placement for her.

Siblings may know before you do that their brother of sister are using. Usually they don't want to "narc" or "rat out" their sibling. They can be a good source of information but this puts them in a very difficult position. First, find a way to validate the information to be sure that they are not trying to get even with their sibling for some prior wrong doing. Be absolutely sure not to disclose personal information shared by the concerned sibling that will identify them as the source. This could have serious repercussions from the addicted sibling who might act out against the "good" child. Other siblings may feel very resentful, angry and disgusted with the amount of time and money you are spending on helping your troubled child. They may feel ignored because they behave and don't require your scrutinizing eye.

I know that my daughter was deeply affected by her older brother's situation. In essence, her big brother had let her down and was no longer a role model. She was very good at keeping the toxic "secrets" that Matt had confided to her on occasion.

Matt tells me that he intentionally let Megan know some of what was going on because he thought by showing the horror of his chaotic life he could insure she would not go down the same path. He has now come to realize that his approach backfired and only served to build a large wall between them. I know Matt's drug abuse had a profound affect on his sister. The chaos Matt's drug use brought into our home affected us all. It occurred during Megan's junior and senior years of gifted high school when the stress of SAT testing, advance placement classes and college application was already looming large. Their sibling relationship is slowly undergoing repair.

This brings up the issue of an individual's physical vulnerability to a substance. One theory is that genetic predisposition accounts for 40-60% chance that they will be affected. It was not until my husband and I entered couples therapy and my husband made the statement, "I hoped Matt would not make the same mistakes that I did" that I discovered there were several of his family members who had addictive disorders, and that during his college years my husband had a serious alcohol problem.

Sometimes marriage is not easy. My husband and I had started couples counseling before the crisis of Matt's illness hit. We were fortunate that we were already seeing the therapist when suddenly thrust into the drama of Matt's drug and mental health issues. She was able to help us work together to care for Matt. That does not mean that we suddenly agreed on every decision. But we did agree to put aside our differences and focus on helping Matt get stable. She warned us that this would be the absolute worst time to separate.

I also learned there were also mental health issues in my husband's family as well. This information was rather shocking to learn after 19 years of marriage. Would this knowledge have changed how I approached the issue or how watchful I would have been of our kid's mental health and possible addictive behaviors. Possibly, but I will never know for sure. Megan at 25 shows no signs of addictive tendencies or depression.

CHAPTER EIGHT
What Do Kids Use?

The answer is............ EVERYTHING!

The following information is a summary of information readily available to you online at the National Institute of Drug Abuse website. This knowledge was invaluable to me as I searched for information and answers. The website provides drug fact sheets on each substance. I have listed the commonly used drugs including street names and a brief description of how they are used and their effects.

CANNEBINOIDS

Drugs in this classification are commonly known as **hashish** (broom, chronic, hash, gangster, oil) and **marijuana** (blunt, dope, ganja, grass, herb, joints, Mary Jane, pot, bud, sensemilla, skunk, weed.) Both of these drugs are ingested or smoked. They produce euphoria, slowed thinking and reaction time, confusion, impaired balance and coordination, impaired memory and learning, increased heart rate, anxiety and panic attacks. Watch for red eyes, cough or frequent respiratory infections. These are definitely gateway drugs which means they very often lead to use of other drugs. Please do not be fooled into thinking that they are drugs of innocent experimentation. Any drug is dangerous. The fact that you may have survived your experimentation in the 60's and 70's without a drug habit does not mean your kid will follow suit. Sometimes we feel inhibited or hypocritical talking about grass because maybe we used when we were young. Push that aside and talk anyway. Times are different and more dangerous than they were in the past.

HALLUCINOGENS

LSD, Lysergicaciddiethylamide, (acid, blotter, boomers, cubes, microdot, yellow sunshines

Mescaline, (buttons, cactus, purple passion, shrooms)

LSD is ingested and absorbed through mouth tissues. Mescaline and mushrooms are swallowed but mescaline can be smoked. These cause altered states of perception and feeling, which often causes nausea. Hallucinogens can also cause flashbacks which is a persisting perception disorder. Matt describes these as "split seconds of feeling high again." These can happen long after the drugs have left the body.

STIMULANTS

Amphetamines (bispetamine, Dexedrine, bennies, black beauties, crosser, hearts, LA turnaround, speed, truck, drivers, uppers.)

These are injected, swallowed, smoked, or snorted. The effects include increased heart rate, increased blood pressure and metabolism, feeling of exhilaration, energy and mental alertness. Watch for rapid or irregular heart rate, reduced appetite and weight loss, nervousness, insomnia, rapid breathing, tremor, irritability anxiousness restlessness, impulsive behavior and aggressiveness.

Cocaine (blow, bump, C, candy, Charlie, coke, chronic, crack, flake, rock, snow, foot.)

This is injected, smoked or snorted. Use can cause sweating, increased temperature, nausea, abdominal pain, stroke, seizure, headache, malnutrition and panic attacks. Watch for mirrors, razorblades and crumpled up foil balls in your teen's room.

Methamphetamines (chalk, crank, crystal, fire, glass, go first, ice, meth, speed).

These are injected, swallowed, smoked, and snorted. Meth can cause aggression, violence, psychotic behavior, or memory loss. Watch for foil balls, black q-tips, broken glass, broken light bulbs, butane lighters and paraphernalia.

MDMA Methylenedioxy-methamphetamine Ecstasy (Also known as adam, clarity, molly, ecstasy, eve, lovers speed, peace, STP, X. XTC.)

This is swallowed and causes mild hallucinogenic effects. It also causes increased tactile sensitivity, empathetic feeling, impaired memory and learning, hyperthermia, cardiac, liver and renal toxicity. Often used at raves. Raves are all night dance parties. Depending on where they are held they may or may not be legal. Drug use is a big part of the "action." In the early days of raves ecstasy was the drug of choice, but now all drugs are represented and available to under age kids.

Ritalin (Jif, MPH, R Ball, skippy, the smart drug, vitamin R.)
Ritalin is swallowed or crushed up and snorted. This is safely used for treatment of Attention Deficit Disorder but kids share it and sell it This is a stimulant and kids can become psychologically and physically addicted to it as they use more and more of it for desired effects.

Adderal This is also safely use for treatment of attention deficit disorder. This has become known as the study drug. It is popular on college campuses. It too is a stimulant and can be compared to speed when it is abused. The pill is generally swallowed. It is perceived as a way to increase concentration and focus while pulling an all-nighter studying. They might experience restlessness, excitability, or anxiety.

BENZODIAZEPINES (ativan, valium, xanax also known as candy, downers, sleeping pills tracks). It is swallowed or injected and causes drowsiness, sedation and dizziness.

METHAQUILONE (Quaalude) Also known as ludes, mandrix, quad, quey. These are swallowed. (Popped) They are used for their sedative effects. Common side effects of Quaaludes include dizziness, nausea, vomiting, diarrhea, abdominal cramps, and fatigue.

OPIODOIDS/MORPHINE DERIVATIVES.
These cause euphoria, drowsiness and sedation. They can also cause confusion, sedation, respiratory depression, tolerance, and addiction, staggering gait. Coma and death can result from overdose. Watch for missing medications in your medicine cabinet!

Codeine is injected or swallowed

Morphine is injected, swallowed or smoked

Oxycontin-swallowed, snorted or, injected

Heroin (black sugar, dope, horse, H, junk, skag, skunk, smack, white horse). These are injected, snorted and smoked. They cause confusion, sedation, respiratory depression, tolerance, addiction, staggering gait, coma and death.

INHALANTS

Solvents (paint thinner, gasoline, and glue)

Gasses (butane, propane, aerosol propellants, nitrous oxide)

These are also known as laughing gas, poppers, snappers and whippets. These are inhaled via the nose or mouth. They cause stimulation and loss of inhibition, slurred speech, and loss of motor coordination. Watch for missing household items like whiteout, markers and air freshener. These cause headaches, chronic congestion "asthma like condition" and red eyes. Excessive use of use of eye drops may be a sign.

HOUSEHOLD ITEMS

Pure vanilla extract and mouth washes are used for the alcohol content. Nutmeg gives a high similar to LSD.

Warning Signs

There are warning signs, some very obvious others more subtle. Personality changes are common. Going from being a nice kid to a mean and angry kid is not normal and should set off alarms. This kind of change can mean many things such as your child is a victim of abuse, bullying, or has a coexisting mental disorder. Watch for clothing and hair changes or sloppy attire. Grooming behaviors may cease to exist. Baggy pants with lots of pockets may now become standard. You may find missing household items, prescriptions medication missing, and little gadgets around their bedroom. Troubled kids tend to ignore household rules, breaking curfew, will not answer cell phone calls, or won't call home. You may feel uneasy about your teen's new friends - LISTEN TO YOUR INNER VOICE.

Weight changes can be related to eating disorders or decreased appetite from speed or cocaine use. Eating binges can be due to marijuana use.

Here are some questions to ask yourself.

- **Is my kid testing the limits at home and breaking family rules?**
- **Is there a change in school performance?... Have there been suspensions?... or bad grades?**
- **Am I comfortable with my kid's friends?**
- **Is personal hygiene slipping beyond your expectation?**

- **Does my kid wear black a lot or wear sloppy attire?**
- **Is my kid manipulative?**
- **Does my kid lack motivation, seem apathetic, or disinterested in life?**
- **Are money or are valuables missing from my home?**
- **Does my kid have temper outbursts?**
- **Do you trust your kid?**

Looking back, I realize now that every one of these signs applied to Matt. I wish I had had a list like this at that time to help me put my feelings into a context. This would have helped me put parts of the puzzle of Matt's situation into a understandable framework.

Overview Of The Various Drugs Teens Use

ALCOHOL AND CIGARETTES

Alcohol and cigarette use by teens are very serious problems. These are proven gateway drugs and pose a huge threat to moving on to other drugs. Alcohol is a depressant and affects the central nervous system while nicotine acts as a stimulant increasing dopamine levels in the brain that lead to craving and addiction. Both are fast acting. Alcohol and cigarettes are very easy for kids to obtain. Widely seen on television and in movies, smoking cigarettes and drinking alcohol appear as normal every day occurrences and it looks cool. Because these are legal behaviors for adults, they see it as a way of asserting independence and appearing mature.

The National Center on Addiction and Substance abuse (CASA) at Columbia University released a study results in 2011 that indicates that nicotine poses a significant risk of damage to the developing brains of teens and can make them more susceptible to alcohol and other drug addictions. The study compared 12-17 year olds who did not smoke with those who did smoke and the comparison shows that smokers are 5 times more likely to drink and 13 times more likely to use marijuana. This study also found that smoking teens were more likely to have experienced symptoms of depression than the non smokers. Smoking at a young age is related to panic attacks, general anxiety disorders and post traumatic stress disorder.

This was definitely the case for Matthew. Following the stressful situation of sexual harassment in his sophomore year of high school he began smoking to "take the edge off" his bad feelings. This very soon led to use of marijuana. Smoking was Matt's gateway drug. Nicotine is one of the most addictive substances available to teens not because of the effect on the brain so much as other drugs, but because of the association with the pleasurable habits that are associated with smoking. Addiction happens quickly.

According to the American Lung association's Smoking and Teens fact sheet, thousands of children under the age of 18 smoke their first cigarette every year. One fourth of them become regular smokers. Lifetime risk is that half will ultimately die of this habit. One third of all smokers had their first cigarette by the age of 14. Ninety percent of smokers begin smoking before age 21.

Tobacco products include: cigarettes, cigars, and smokeless tobacco. In addition there are other products used by kids including, pipes, bidis (small, hand rolled cigarettes flavored like candy) and Kretekes, which are clove cigarettes.

Alcohol is the most widely used drug in the United States, teen or adult. Teens have many misconceptions about alcohol. They see it as a way to loosen up, look cool, or a way to fit in. Again, the media and movies play a big part in stimulating teen interest in alcohol. Alcohol seems harmless to teens based on what they have seen on television and in movies, and perhaps even in their own home when parents consume alcohol.

Adolescence is a time of transition and kids want to fit in with their friends so going along with the crowd is a natural response and this is when many kids are introduced to alcohol. Alcohol is absorbed quickly into the blood stream from the lining of the stomach and the effects last for several hours depending on how much and how quickly it is consumed. Females absorb alcohol faster than males because the water content in their body is less than in males. According to the National Center on Addiction and Substance abuse 80% of high school students have tried alcohol.

Alcohol is often referred to as booze, sauce, brews, brewskies, hooch, hard stuff and juice. If you think your kid has not been exposed then you may be hiding your head in the sand. According to CASA, one third of teens and nearly half of all 17 year olds go to parties at friends' homes where parents are present and teens are using alcohol or drugs. So, the fact that adults are in the home does not insure a substance free party. When parents are not present, alcohol and drugs are even more likely to be there. Half of teen report that alcohol and drugs are present at parties and 80 % of parents believe that neither of these substances are available. 98% of parents who were surveyed report being home when there are parties and 33% of teens say parents are never or rarely present at parties. We need to be more alert to the presence of alcohol and other drugs. Our denial or lack of awareness puts our kids at risk of drinking and using drugs.

The consequences of teen alcohol abuse are potentially catastrophic when drinking and driving occur. In 2004 the National Highway Traffic Safety Administration reported that 29% of drivers killed in motor vehicle crashes had been drinking. Traffic crashes are the leading cause of death in teens. Physical fights, and falls increase with alcohol. Alcohol poisoning is a constant threat to teens.

MARIJUANA

Marijuana is made from the leaves of cannabis plants (hemp) seed, stem, buds and flowers. There are over 200 slang terms for marijuana. You may hear: pot, herb, grass, weed, bud, Mary Jane, reefer, ganja, broom, Texas tea, Maui wowie just to name some of the more commonly heard terms. Marijuana of today is much more potent than the weed of the 1960's. It is often laced with PCP or cocaine and is highly addictive. There is new evidence demonstrating it may be physically addicting as well. The National Institute of Drug Abuse reports that marijuana is the illegal drug most used in this country. Studies show nearly 50% of teens try it before they graduate from high school. In addition, marijuana use now starts at a younger age making teens and some pre teens more likely to become dependent on it or another drug later in life. Parents in the two states where marijuana was just legalized in the 2012 election, for recreational use and medical marijuana states need to be more vigilant.

The active ingredient in marijuana is THC (tetrahydrocannabinal). THC enters the lungs, and then flows through the blood stream to other body organs and the brain. It affects canaboid receptors in the brain that influence pleasure, memory and thought. It is mind altering and psychoactive. Marijuana can induce relaxation and introspection. Within minutes of inhaling the user starts to feel high or is filled with pleasant sensations. TCH triggers brain cells to release dopamine — creating good feelings for a short time. This leads to the urge to smoke again and again and again. Short term effects include motor coordination impairment, problems with memory and learning, and distorted perception. Depression, anxiety and personality disturbances have been associated with use of marijuana because of its effect on dopamine. The only treatment available is behavioral. No medications are available for treatment.

Why do kids choose to use weed? It is easy to get from school mates, older siblings, or friends. Peer pressure plays a big role. Smoking weed is often made to "look cool" in movies and TV. Kids often see marijuana as a way to cope with life's problems such as anxiety, depression, to escape from reality, or ease boredom. Teens do not perceive "pot" as dangerous. BEWARE, THIS IS A GATEWAY DRUG. Please start talking to your kids by the age of 12.

Marijuana is usually hand rolled in cigarette papers called joints. It can be used in pipes or water pipes called a bong. Blunts are hollowed out cigars stuffed with marijuana and often combined with cocaine. Sometimes it is made into a tea or cooked into food like "special" brownies.

Kids high on this drug appear dizzy, may have trouble walking, and they may seem silly or giggly for no reason. Blood shot eyes, excessive use of eye drops and difficulty remembering things that just happened are warning signs. Watch for pipes, rolling paper, and body odor. Teens use incense, cologne, or perfume to hide body odor. Matt would often rub incense sticks on his shirts, a behavior I thought odd, but, when asked why he did it he said it was because he didn't like cologne. Sometimes kids will use room deodorizers.

The use of synthetic marijuana, or spice, also known as K2, is on the rise. Until early in 2011 this was legally sold. In 2011 one out of nine high school seniors (11.4%) report using spice in the preceding 12 months. It produces effects similar to marijuana; elevated mood, relaxation, and altered perception are common. In some cases it is stronger than marijuana. Some users report effects of extreme anxiety, paranoia and hallucinations. Other effects might be a rapid heart rate, vomiting, agitation, confusion, decreased circulation of blood to the heart resulting in cardiac arrest. It is not known how spice affects health in the long run or how toxic it may be. It may contain harmful metal residues.

Matt started smoking weed to ease the pain of a situation of sexual harassment at school. For some unknown reason an athletic team mate started a rumor that Matt was gay and this spread throughout his school of 4500 students. Teens can be so cruel. He was known as the "team faggot." He was harassed on the bus on the way home from sports games or while sitting at the bus stop after school. He was often followed down the hallway at school hearing derogatory names being called out by his team mates as they followed him to class. Sometimes strangers would ask him if he was "that gay guy" at school.

At the age of 16, developmentally, adolescents are trying to figure out who they are and Matt also had to show who he wasn't. This triggered a situational depressive event which led him to use marijuana to ease the pain. This was his first attempt at "self medicating." He began smoking cigarettes as well. Suddenly he no longer fit into main stream high school and sought out different friends.

I remember a night that Matt called from a new friend's house asking to spend the night. Spending the night was an unusual request and it set off my internal parental alarms. This was someone I did not know so I insisted that he come home. I sensed that something was off because he seemed uncharacteristically happy and silly when he arrived home. He denied drug or alcohol use, and we could uncover no concrete proof, so we let it slide with a lecture. But ultimately it left us uneasy. This is what triggered my interest in cleaning his room several days later and led to my finding remnants of marijuana and cigarettes hidden in his room. This was the beginning of Matt's journey into the darkness of drug abuse.

HALLUCINOGENS

"Follow me down the rabbit hole"
~ Matt

Hallucinogens are drugs that cause distortion in the user's perception of reality. People see images, hear sounds and have sensations, all seeming real at the time, but in reality do not exist. Hallucinogens disrupt the interaction of neuron cells in the brain and serotonin. LSD, peyote, and mushrooms are the most recognizable members of this class of drugs. Also related are dissociative drugs like PCP and Ketamine (special K) which were first developed as surgical anesthetics. They cause the user to feel detached or disassociated from their surroundings. Historically hallucinogens have been around thousands of years, often used in shamanictic and religious rituals and to provoke mystical insight.

LSD users report feelings of altered sense of time and space. In addition there may be rapid emotional swings which can cause panic feelings or "bad trips." Mushrooms have LSD like properties. They cause hallucinations, altered sense of time, and difficulty separating reality from fantasy. Panic reactions can occur. Physical signs of use may be dilated pupils, increased heart rate, sweating, decreased appetite, or loss of muscle coordination.

The NIDA states that 4% of 12th graders reported use of LSD in 2008. About 7% of high school seniors reported life time use of other hallucinogens. Roughly 1% of high school seniors reported using PCP.

SALVIA: a pot like hallucinogen
Starting in 2008, attention began to be focused on a commonly found herb, Salvia divinarum. At that time he National Survey on Drug Use indicated 1.8 million people 12 or older have used salvia. This is a hallucinonogenic herb. It is a member of the mint family. Dried leaves are smoked or chewed or the extract made into a drink. It produces a high lasting 1-30 minutes. Psychedelic like changes, visual perception, mood and body sensations, and emotional swings may occur. No concrete studies exist to show lasting effects or potential for addiction. This has

become an issue for many states where legislation has been passed concerning the use and possession of salvia. California, North Dakota, Illinois, Delaware and Missouri are among them. This herb is felt to be like LSD. Regulatory control exists in many countries. Long term effects have not been investigated. The DEA lists this as a drug of concern.

Monitoring the Future studies in 2011 indicate 1.6% of eighth graders, 3.9% of 10 graders and 5.9% of twelfth graders have used salvia. It has gained popularity with teens. The Substance Abuse and Mental Health Services Administration (SAMSA) in 2008 estimated 1.8 million people age 12 and older have used this in their lifetime. It is most common in young adults age 18-25. It is grown domestically and imported from Mexico, Central and South America. The internet is used for promotion. People who use salvia may experience hallucinations or delusional episodes. Effects are psychedelic like and cause changes in perception of vision or body sensations.

Matt's use of hallucinogens

Although Matt tried salvia once or twice he really doesn't remember much about it. Other hallucinogens like mushrooms, acid, and PCP followed his use of marijuana and they were apparently memorable. Matt remembers dropping acid at high school because it was easy to get ahold of. He also found this made school "more interesting" and it helped him "pass the time." Matt said he used this type of drug for about a year before moving on to methamphetamines. By the time he moved into his senior year of high school he had progressed from cigarettes and alcohol to marijuana followed by hallucinogens and finally culminating with methamphetamines and heroin. Matt says this progression is not unusual for teens heavily involved with drug use.

HUFFING

"F* huffing, I wanna get high not kill brain cells."**
~ Matt

There are many "innocent" household products that when inhaled cause a mind-altering effect. Depending on the type of chemical, teens feel different effects. Huffing is on the rise with youth. There are 3 ways kids use inhalants. Huffing is accomplished by soaking a rag in the inhalant and pressing the rag to the mouth to breath. Sniffing means to sniff or snort fumes from an aerosol container and bagging means inhaling fumes sprayed into a plastic or paper bag. Watch for new behaviors like purchasing hairspray, nail polish, nail polish remover or whipped cream. All of these seen seem pretty innocent, right? WRONG. These are just a few of the substances that kids huff. Huffing can harm the liver, kidney, bone marrow and brain.

These chemical can be divided up into three categories:
- **Solvents**
- **Gasses**
- **Nitrites.**

Solvents: paint thinner, nail polish remover, degreasers, gasoline, glue, correction fluid (white out) and felt tip markers.

Gasses: butane lighters, propane tanks, whipped cream dispensers, spray paint, hair spray, deodorant spray, fabric protector spray

Nitrites: Room deodorizers, butyl nitrite (used in perfume and antifreeze — now illegal)

National surveys say that kids as young as fourth grade have huffed at least once. NIDA research of 8th, 10th, and 12th graders show that in 2010 kids who used at least once numbered 8.1% in 8th grade, 5.7% in 10th grade and 3.6% in 12 grade.

You might notice a chemical smell on their body or clothes, correction fluid on fingers or noses, possession of ample markers, red eyes, strange breath odor, headaches, sores around their mouth, and of course poor grades in school. Also be on the lookout for empty paint cans, paint stains on clothing or in the bedroom, slurred speech, and disoriented appearance. Huffing was not one of Matt's substances of choice.

COCAINE

"Coke---f* that, why bother with a 20 minute high
when I can smoke speed and get spun for hours."**
~ Matt

Cocaine is powerfully addictive, stimulating the central nervous system. Cocaine produces euphoric effects and there is an immediate rush lasting only a few minutes. The heart beats faster, metabolism speeds up and the user may appear more talkative and energetic or anxious. Dopamine is affected by cocaine in such a way that in early use there is a good feeling but over time with repeated use the dopamine reaction is dulled and no pleasure is felt. The user then needs to use more and more to experience a pleasurable feeling.

Long term use can lead to panic attacks, irritability, and anxiety. There is also the possibility of full blown paranoia and psychotic breaks.
Violent behavior, insomnia, and confusion are seen in heavy users with the risk of sudden cardiac arrest and death. Cocaine is commonly combined with other drugs, like alcohol, which increases the risk for sudden death.

In 2009, 4.8 million Americans age 12 and older reported using cocaine. One and one half million had used crack cocaine. Monitoring the Future 2010, reports that when asked about cocaine use during the past twelve months, 1.6% of eighth graders, 2.2% of tenth graders and 2.9% of high school seniors admitted to using crack cocaine.

Cocaine is used by snorting through the nose which sends it to the blood stream. Its use can cause damage to the sinuses and teeth. It can also be injected which presents other problems like exposure to hepatitis and AIDS from shared needles. Sometimes it is mixed with other drugs like heroin and cooked or smoked in a glass pipe. People using cocaine often have red, blood shot eyes, a runny nose, frequent sniffing and weight loss.

Crack cocaine is processed cocaine. This is done so that it can be smoked. It looks like small shavings of soap. (But sharp like shards of glass) Crack cocaine gets to the brain faster than cocaine powder. Unfortunately there are no FDA approved medications for the treatment of cocaine abuse.

METHAMPHETAMINES

"A tweaker will steal your stuff then help you look for it."
~ Annon.

"This filled needle is my unsharpened sword.
I stab but cannot puncture.
I don't want to feel much longer.
Please make me numb once again."
~ Matt

To this day just thinking or hearing something in the news about methamphetamines is very upsetting to me. It triggers flashbacks to the terrible time when we discovered Matt was using. I believe that you never really get over the fact that your kid is a drug addict. Even in recovery there is that feeling that it could end at any time. According to the National Institute on Drug Abuse, methamphetamines are highly addictive; a stimulant related to amphetamine but which is longer lasting and more toxic in its effect on the central nervous system. There is high potential for abuse and addiction.

Meth causes alterations in the activity of the neurotransmitter system of the brain. It increases release of high levels of dopamine and stimulates brain cells enhancing mood and stimulating body movement. There is a boost in activity of neurotransmitters followed by a speed crash which often causes the drug user to use other drugs to counteract the withdrawal and in turn establishes a cross addiction. The National Survey of Drug Use and Health (NSDUH) 2009 stated that 1.2 million Americans 12 and older have tried meth at least once in their lifetime. The typical user was once white, male and blue collar. This is not true today as it affects a diverse population. Methamphetamines were first introduced in the 1930's as an asthma treatment and used until the mid 1960's when it began to be used for more recreational purposes.

The federal government then classified it as a restricted narcotic. The speed freaks of the 1960's found that it gave a stand-a-lone fix with consistent highs. I remember a slogan from my younger days related to the Flower Children of the 60's: "Speed Kills" a feeble attempt at best in educating youth about the dangers of speed. Of course street chemists found a way to make it and each decade since, the cooking methods have been refined and made easier. Sad to say that today anyone can go on the internet and get a recipe for meth and instructions for setting up a "lab."

In 2010, the NIDA Monitoring the Future Study reports that 1.2% of 8th graders, 1.6% of 10th graders and 1.0% of high school seniors had abused meth at least once prior to the survey. Most teens obtain meth from friends and acquaintances. Typically the distribution is closed and somewhat hidden in prearranged locations by networking. It is easy for the average high school student to find the local peer supplier. Meth causes altered judgment and inhibition leading to unsafe behaviors like shared needles, and unplanned, unprotected sex which leads to increased rates of diseases like HIV, sexually transmitted infections, and hepatitis.

Meth users are called "tweakers." The origin of this name is unclear; however, there are 2 "urban legend" explanations. This may be a shortened version of "two weekers" indicating that tweakers often remain sleepless for long periods of time. Another thought is it refers to the fact that when high, tweakers will tinker with gadgets and tweak them incessantly but not really produce any results. Matt did strange things with duct tape using it to "build" book shelves or hang sheets up in his room for "privacy." Meth is readily available, cheep to buy, and produces an extended high that is attractive to the young and foolish. It speeds up the central nervous system which, according to Matt, is pleasurable and decreases the need for sleep. Euphoric feelings may be increased as well as the sex drive. It literally burns the body and mind up because of the accelerated metabolism.

Instant effects include wakefulness, physical activity, and decreased appetite. Heart rate, respiration, and blood pressure increase. Over time you may observe irritability, anxiety insomnia, confusion and tremors. Long term use can even lead to psychiatric disorders. It is highly toxic due to the chemicals used to illegally manufacture it and lasting effects may include paranoia, aggressiveness, extreme anorexia, memory loss, hallucinations, delusions and stroke.

"Meth mouth" is also a common occurrence which is a severe dental disease where by teeth and gums are permanently destroyed.

More noticeable signs in your teen might be agitation, excited speech, decreased appetite or weight loss, and increased physical activity. Dilated pupils, shortness of breath, and nausea and vomiting are often signs of use.

I remember times when Matt just wouldn't sleep at night, staying up to "work on art projects for college." He would paint very grotesque creatures, but often using vivid colors and hiding a message of despair or in some cases hope or love in his work. He was very creative with duck tape and frequently wrote in a journal. I later read some of his entries while he was hospitalized and they were frightening. When Matt was in rehab and we were getting his room ready for his return, I found his hidden journal. He would describe hallucinations and physical symptoms in such great detail that I just couldn't handle reading in large doses.

I vividly remember the day I came home from work to find that Matt had used spray paint to make his bedroom window black. He said he did it because his room was not dark enough for sleep. I can't describe the feelings this triggered. I knew something was horribly amiss. He had also brought a cinder block to use as a door barrier. I remember having to force his door open to get into his room because of the cinderblock. His explanation was he wanted to be able to have privacy. It was only after reading his journal while he was in rehab that I discovered that this was done during a paranoid attack where he thought a SWAT team was outside the house. He felt the need to barricade himself in his room feeling absolutely certain they would burst into his room at any minute. On another occasion I came home to find Matt had used spray paint to put graffiti type quotes on his wall. He said that these were serious thoughts that he was pondering. It read:"To every beginning there comes an end but what if the end is truly the beginning and beginnings have no end?" I will never forget my completely overwhelming feelings of fear and helplessness in each of those situations.

Methamphetamine labs are found even in the best communities. These are a huge environmental hazard. They can be very dangerous and some have exploded. Generally there are strong chemical smells like ammonia or fuel in the surrounding neighborhood. If you get close enough, you might see laboratory equipment like glass tubing, beakers, or Bunsen burners. Large plastic containers might be seen in the yard. Watch for windows covered with plastic, foil, wood, tarps, or other materials. Hoses hanging out from a window are also a bad sign.

Look for large quantities (cans or drums) in the yard. These are generally Drano, iodine crystals, pool acid (notable especially if there is no pool) or large bags of kitty litter. People may stand outside only long enough to smoke and automobile or foot traffic may increase and look suspicious. Frequently bars on the windows and surveillance cameras or high fences are used to protect the lab. Meth is more available than you think and it's important to educate yourself on what to look for in order to keep your teen safe.

Matt tells me he would get so high nothing else mattered. All those feelings of sadness and anger were replaced with euphoria. He said he felt like the energizer bunny and thought he could conquer the world. Oddly Matt never broke curfew and appeared for meals. What I did not know was he did this only so we would think everything was OK. Unknown to me he would eat in front of us but then throw it all up afterwards. Matt says after a while you don't smoke to get high you smoke to get normal. You're in total agony if you don't get your morning hit. Without meth Matt would get "dope sick, feeling physically horrible, and becoming irritable.

Little did I know Matt would go long periods of time without sleep. He remembers going a week and a half with no sleep. It was during this time he would see speed "demons" sitting in his room. He did paintings of these hallucinations. A hallucination is what prompted him to spray paint his windows black thinking a SWAT team was outside his room.

Matt says methamphetamines produced the worst mental addiction for him. The come downs were the worst because he would be tired and would want to sleep but the craving was horrible so he would do more. He wasn't eating and lost 50 pounds which was hidden by layered clothes. He would bounce back and forth from depression when he came down off the drug to mania when he was using . Heroin use followed.

HEROIN

"The spike runs everything."
~ Matt

Just the thought of teens using this drug puts fear into the minds of parents. The memory of Matt using heroin still makes me anxious and unsettled 8 years after the fact. Many parents have no idea that teens use this hard core drug. This is a highly addictive drug and a serious problem in America. Heroin is processed from morphine. It appears as a white or brown paper. Street names are smack, H, or Junk — hence the name junkie. One who uses heroin is labeled a junkie. Its use is associated with serious health conditions. HIV/AIDS and hepatitis are also serious risks for heroin users who share needles. Fatal overdose can happen.

Unfortunately movies and television stories often may seem to glamorize the lives of famous users who have died of overdoses. This can be deadly for teens. Many of Mathew's favorite musical idols died of drug overdose. Matt told me he always wondered why someone who seemed to have great life would throw their life away for a drug. That curiosity made him want to experience this drug at least once in his life. At some point he knew he would try it at least once. He did, but not just once, he continued to use until his arrest for possession.

Oddly, I am relieved that Matt knew where to go to find a needle exchange program and did not share needles (that he can recall). This showed awareness on a certain level of the risks he was taking. Matt is a smart kid and I'm thankful that some of the health messages I gave both of my children as they moved into their teen years were remembered. Granted, I did not talk specifically about needle exchange programs but general health, safe sex and substance abuse were covered. I remember looking into his back pack once and finding syringes. I felt physically ill and confronted him. He said, and I stupidly believed him, that he had confiscated them from a "friend" to prevent him from using. This illustrates how desperately I wanted to believe Matt was ok.

Short term effects occur soon after a dose and disappear in a few hours. After injection or ingestion there is a surge of euphoria called a "rush." This is followed by a period of wakeful drowsiness called "on the nod" Chronic use collapses veins, can cause heart infections, abscesses, cellulitis, and liver disease. Street heroin has impurities that don't dissolve and can cause serious long term health effects.

Tolerance develops quickly which means the junkie needs more and more to attain the same effects. Overdose and death may follow the ever increasing need for more. Withdrawal can happen within hours of use causing craving, restlessness, nausea, and bone pain. Treatment options include the use of medications like methadone, bupernerpine or naltrexone. Behavioral therapies are essential.

The 2010 The Monitoring the Future Study indicated that approximately 0.8% of eighth and tenth grade students surveyed, and 0.9% of twelfth graders had used heroin at least once during the past twelve months.. The results for 2007 did not change significantly.

Matt has been very honest about his experience with heroin and this honesty is frightening. Matt says, "Injecting heroin is the most addictive way to do it. The high is so much more incredible than if you were to smoke it or snort it. There is absolutely no way a user can describe the feeling heroin creates. It has a way of taking the entire world's ugliness and making everything beautiful. There is absolutely no way of creating the feeling of using without the drug." This honesty underscores the fact that relapse can happen at any time. For this reason I am hyper vigilant about Matt's wellbeing. Matt says that heroin users often remember the exact feeling years, even decades later of how they felt on heroin. This is unlike any other drug. It is with sadness and fear that I realize that Matt will always remember this feeling.

As the years have passed since Matt used heroin he has shared other frightening information, always careful to ask "Are you sure you want to know mom?" Matt says as soon as he tried it he was hooked. He started smoking it but rapidly progressed to injecting it into his arm. He said at that point he was a full blown junkie and will be for the rest of his life. He says he can never let his guard down.

The statement that follows is the most powerful messages you will ever read, "Nothing on this planet is powerful enough to destroy the bliss I felt after shooting up. I will never forget how good it felt. I now know why people would throw their life away for a drug. Heroin consumes you and changes you in a way you don't realize until it is too late and your life is taken away." As I read these words today the profoundly sad feeling of being the parent of an addict returns.

CHAPTER NINE

Principles of Drug Addiction Treatment

**"If you let yourself go and open your mind
then you'll reach a point called being free."**

~ Matt

Drug abuse is a complex but treatable brain disease. It is compulsive craving and seeking. The use happens even when there are negative effects. It is a chronic relapsing disease. One might even compare it to chronic diseases like diabetes or asthma. If uncontrolled these can have dire consequences. The goal is to enable the user to achieve lasting abstinence but more immediately the goal needs to be to reduce the drug abuse, improve functioning, and minimizing negative health and social effects. Treatment needs to help addicts change destructive behavior to avoid relapse and remove themselves from a life of addiction.

The NIDA has identified fundamental principles that characterize effective drug abuse treatment. These can be found on their website. I have paraphrased and summarized them below.

- **No single method of treatment works for every person**
- **Treatment needs to be easy to get to.**
- **Treatment needs to look at the whole person.**
- **As treatment progresses individual needs change. There is no specifically prescribed time frame for treatment, each person is different**
- **Individual counseling, group counseling and other behavioral therapies are all very important parts of effective treatment.**
- **Medications are needed by many addicts and may be an important part of therapy, especially when they are combined with counseling and behavioral therapies.**
- **Addicts and drug abusing individuals who also have a mental health**

disorder should have both problems treated.

- **Medical detoxification is only the first stage of addiction treatment and by itself does little to change long term drug use.**
- **Treatment does not need to be voluntary to be effective. Possible drug use even during treatment must be monitored continuously.**
- **Treatment programs should provide assessment for HIV/AIDS, hepatitis B & C and tuberculosis.**
- **Drug abuse treatment is a long term process and the addict needs on going support.**

So what does all this mean? Many programs exist to treat drug abuse. Perhaps the best known of these are 12 Step programs like Alcoholics Anonymous, Cocaine Anonymous and Narcotics Anonymous. These are self help group support programs that have proven to be quite effective in treatment. The twelve step programs attempt to remove denial and expose pain thus encouraging healing. Many other options are available to you and can be accessed trough referral by your pediatrician, family practice doctor, clergy or school district. Other options are individualized or group counseling, hospital based services, residential treatment centers, and addiction rehabilitation centers.

Getting help from an addiction medical specialist is often necessary and I urge you to look into this for your teen. In general it is essential to determine the level of care your kid needs. You can find referrals in your community. Your personal physician or health plan can help you find local resources. The American Society of Addiction Medicine (www.ASAM.org) or the American Academy of Addiction Psychiatry (www.AAAP.org) are available online and offer suggestions.

What follows is a summary of the kinds of treatments available.

Long term treatment involves 30 days or more of continuous treatment depending on the level of addiction and how the teen is functioning in his world.

Inpatient acute care is for the severely impaired addicts requiring complicated withdrawal or treatment for medical or mental health issues as well.

Non-hospital residential treatment removes the addict from the environment but generally this does not include medical treatment for existing diseases. (diabetes, mental health diagnosis etc.)

Partial hospital intensive treatment is used if it is safe to stay in their current environment but need intense daily supervision.

Outpatient treatments are for more stable individuals who need minimal monitoring. Generally certified addiction counselors, psychologists, and clinical social workers, conduct individual and group meetings to discuss problems.

Twelve step programs are supplements to all these programs or may stand alone. These are member run group sessions. The addict must admit that they are powerless over their addiction and rely on their "higher power" to help them through the process of recovery.

Long term residential treatment may be necessary. These are free standing centers that guide the addict to work towards responsibility. This may take months or years. Group therapy, education, and vocational counseling are included.

Ongoing after care is essential and necessary to prevent relapse. Family involvement should be a big part of treatment. Random drug testing is useful in determining if your teen is still using. Most commonly used are urine tests that can detect amphetamines and cocaine for 2-3 days after use and opiates 1-3 days after use. These test kits have become readily available in the retail settings. Keep in mind there are ways that addicts can change the results of the test. Many web sites exist that explain how to beat drug testing. These include sites that sell urine. In the case of one who must be observed providing a urine sample there are intricate bags and tubes that can be strapped on to a leg to provide "clean samples." They can also get a clean friend to give them a sample of their urine. Sometimes bleach is added to a urine sample. According to Matt "head shops" (places to buy drug paraphernalia) also sell detox drinks and other products.

Early in his court ordered recovery Matt went to 12 step meetings irregularly,

Chemical Dependency Recovery Program meetings irregularly, day treatment programs, you name it, he tried it. He was looking for the easy way out. Be advised there is NO EASY WAY! Matt, due to his arrest, was required to attend court ordered drug education and testing meetings for first time offenders. In California it is called PC1000. He tells me that after the meeting often they would get high. He said this was a great place to score drugs.

The participants had also figured out when testing would occur and always seemed to be clean on that night. Matt also told me that some 12 step meetings can be a source for obtaining drugs. It is very important to choose meetings wisely. I believe (my bias) is that the best course of action when discovering your kid is using is to force them into a live in situation. This works well if your kid is under 18 years of age, and has health insurance, but, once 18 they can refuse treatment.

I now see that we enabled Matt to use way longer than we should have, but, I was totally afraid that kicking him out of the house would serve no purpose other than sending him into the arms of drug dealers and user friends. I truly believe he would have become a homeless, crazy, street person with an untreated mental disorder. We probably would have had to identify Matt in a morgue had we taken this approach. I felt strongly that Matt was deep down a good kid, hugely troubled with a mental illness he was trying to deal with by self-medicating, but definitely not a "throw away."

Although my husband and I agreed that we needed to get Matt treated, we often disagreed on the direction. I tended to take a softer approach than him. He came from the perspective of a recovering alcoholic remembering what he had done in his youth. This created marital stress.

Addicts need to be removed from their familiar environment including people, places, and sometime certain sounds to begin effective treatment. Matthew tried many different programs before we finally had to institute a "Tough Love" intervention in the context of a counseling session. This was another extremely painful night as a parent of a drug abuser. With the help of Matt's therapist, we had pre-arranged an intervention which would result in his admission that evening to a live in program.

The Intervention

During the session we informed Matt that he could no longer live in our home if he continued on his current path. He got angry and refused. Defiantly he informed us that he would move out tonight. What a gut wrenching statement that was! We asked for his keys stating that one of us would drive him home. We told him that he no longer had the privilege of the car since he would not be living at home. He defiantly stated he would drive home and we told him that if he was not home in 45 minutes we would report the car stolen. He left and of course stopped at a supplier's house on the way home for a fix. He arrived home angry, went to his room, and began packing. I was devastated. I actually cried the entire 40 minute trip home from the counselor's office.

Desperate in my fearful and tearful state I looked for a solution. I was afraid that we would never see Matt again. I remembered a woman that Matt had connected with in one of his day programs. Dee had come to our house for dinner several times. Both of them were diagnosed with bipolar disorder and addiction. She had been living with it for 40 years and told Matt she made many mistakes over the years and acted as a big sister to him during this phase of his recovery. Sadly, she had a sister who committed suicide. (The sister was Matt's age at the time of the suicide.) I think this is one of the things that brought Matt and Dee together while they were attending the same mental health day program.

In my desperation, I called Dee and told her what was going on and asked if she would talk to Matt. We pretended that she had randomly called Matt and they spoke for what seemed like an eternity. Matt walked out of his room and to our great relief said that he realized he needed to go into the treatment center or he would be dead! Dee, our family angel, had helped Matt see how bad thing really were. Matt was admitted the next day to a dual diagnosis program where he began a four month stay and his recovery. His initial plan was to stay only one month and continue his lifestyle. But the program got to him and after each month passed by he decided to stay another.

We continued to speak to Dee off and on over the next year during his recovery, but, eventually lost contact with her. I believe people are sent into our lives at certain life cross roads to help with difficult situations. She was definitely sent into our lives to help Matt get on the road to recovery. She was a neutral voice of reason that could tell Matt he needed to clean up and he listened to her. To this day, I feel Dee was the major influence on Matt's entry into rehab. I hope she knows how special she is to our family.

I believe it is helpful to have adult friends or relatives you can call on to be a non parental voice of reason. I am sure many of the things Dee told Matt that night were not unlike what was said at his intervention counseling session. But they weren't coming from us and apparently they got through better than anything we could have said.

While Matt was in this program a sense of peace came over me. He was safe. I did not obsess daily about his whereabouts or worry he was using. With each visit we made he seemed to be getting better. The environment was very structured. His first job there was cleaning toilets. Eventually he worked his way up to cook and helped to create new menu items. The head of the kitchen was a wonderful woman who had a very positive effect on Matt's progress. She was very supportive to us as well giving us feed back that she could see the good kid underneath all the layers of dysfunction and that it was evident Matt had received good messages as a kid and those were beginning to shine through. He attended group sessions during the day. As time progressed he was allowed to go on field trips with residents and staff supervisors. Often they went to community 12 step meetings. We visited on the weekends and even brought the family dog to one visit. What a reunion!

Matt could not have visitors or phone privileges for the first few weeks. But after the initial period of isolation he began calling home to report his progress. The residents of this program were age of 19 up. Many of the older residents told Matt (and us) how lucky he was to have a family that supported him. The staff also said much of Matt's success was due to our participation. Many of the staff members were former addicts and were great role models as well very resistant to manipulation. They knew all the tricks. Matt asked up to bring his macramé and beads up to him so he had a creative outlet. He made jewelry that he sold for a few dollars allowing him to buy things like candy from the "camp store."

We visited Matt weekly while he was at the rehab facility. On one occasion we took the family dog with us. It was a great reunion. Early in Matt's depression we adopted Paco as a therapy dog for him. They were best buddies. However, oddly at one point, Paco abruptly stopped sleeping in Matt's room at night. This was during Matt's heavy drug use time. Even the dog new Matt was using before I did!

This wild ride began February 1, 2004, and was without a doubt the worst day of my life. In contrast, almost two years later, November 4, 2005 was one of the best days of my life. This was the day that Matthew entered a social model recovery program for his dual diagnosis of drug addiction and bipolar disorder. Agreeing to stay one month, he decided each month to extend his stay and ultimately lived in this isolated community for 4 months. He got clean, gained some insight into his condition, was stabilized on medications for his bipolar disorder and began to live again. This was a great start towards sobriety. I emphasize START. It was in this intense 12 step program where he learned to admit he was an addict and would need lifelong support.

Addicts in recovery need support and the positive influence of others. I believe that programs that use former addicts are most useful because these recovery specialists have lived it and don't fall victim to the manipulation addicts are so good at. The addict must demonstrate some willingness to change and admit that there is a problem. Change is usually stimulated by the fact that their addiction is threatening them with a loss. The threat of a lost job, spouse, or house may motivate an adult. But the threat of jail time, loss of cars, loss of cell phones, loss of living at home, loosing a driver's license, or seeing a friend die of an overdose might motivate a teenager.

Initially the motivation can come from outside the drug user but as time goes by it needs to change to an internal motivational force. In other words, outside motivation may stimulate the first step, but internal self motivation must follow.

Immediately after picking Matt up from jail we, as his parents, were highly motivated to initiate therapy. Matt was not. Just because he got arrested it did not mean that he was ready for rehab. He had not hit rock bottom yet. That would not happen for many months.

During his abuse Matt interacted with other drug abusers, dope dealers, and even gang members who sold him his drugs. He saw friends die, friends get arrested, friends disappear, and friends become homeless. This was all between the ages of 18 and 20. Often when we talk about the past Matt will ask me, "Do you really want to know?" He knows that these stories affect me deeply and I thank God daily that Matt is alive and willing to tell me about his past life.

CHAPTER TEN

National Studies About Teens and Drug Use

"When ignorance reigns, life is lost."
~ Matt

The most significant study about teens and drug use is done on a regular basis by the University of Michigan and sponsored by the National Institute on Drug Abuse. This is a study of behavior, attitudes and values of American secondary school students, college students and young adults. In 2011, 46,700 teens were asked to provide information about issues surrounding drug use. Overall illicit drug use by American teens has continued a gradual decline since 2002. The studies show a continued small decline in the use of amphetamines, Ritalin, methamphetamines, Adderall and crystal methamphetamine.

Marijuana use among teens rose in 2011 with daily marijuana use at a 30-year peak level among high school seniors. Synthetic marijuana (spice) was used by one in every nine high school seniors in the preceding 12 months.

One drug in particular that has gained in popularity is MDMA (ecstasy). An increase in use has shown up in the upper grades. Over the counter cough and cold medicines are also being used by kids to get high. The ingredient dextromethorphen is one active ingredient teens look for.

Drugs that have held steady in their use include: LSD, hallucinogens other than LSD, salvia, heroin, narcotics other than heroin, and oxycotin. Club drugs such as Rophyponal, GHB, and Ketamine (drugs that cause amnesia and are known as date rape drugs) continue to be used. Methamphetamine, crystal meth, Provigil (a prescription drug used to treat narcolepsy) and anabolic steroids continue to be used as well.

It is interesting to note that there is a continuous flow of new drugs into the scene and older drugs are being rediscovered by today's youth. This phenomenon is called "generational forgetting." It is based on the fact that use of some drugs decrease because of the risks associated with them causing fear. Some drugs make a comeback because the perceived risk of these drugs has been forgotten. Examples of these drugs are inhalants, ecstasy and LSD.

Alcohol use and occasions of heavy drinking continued a long-term gradual decline among teens, reaching historically low levels in 2011. Energy drinks are being consumed by one third of teens with the highest use in younger teens.

CHAPTER ELEVEN
Dual Diagnosis
Mental Health Issues

"There is nothing to lose when no one knows your name.
Would anyone notice if I died today."
~ Matt

One reason teens use is because of pre-existing mental conditions. Adolescence is a time of major change and it might be easy to overlook signs of mental illness and brush it off as teenage immaturity and angst. As parents perhaps we don't want to admit our kid is less than 100% normal. Often we believe kids use drugs or alcohol to rebel or fit in. However, undiagnosed emotional and behavioral problems may cause a kid to use drugs as a way to ease their emotional pain or frustration. It is extremely important to contact a mental health professional who specializes in treatment of adolescents to evaluate your teen and determine a diagnosis.

Matthew was very good at hiding signs of his bipolar disorder although I'm sure on a conscious level he did not know that he was mentally ill. He maintains to this day that from a young age he always felt different and never really fit in. He was very adept at manipulation of his parents, counselors, and physicians. He kept many details of his life out of the therapy sessions and hidden from us. On a certain level Matt knew he was different, and during his junior and senior year of high school he tried to convince us that he had attention deficit disorder (ADD). In retrospect this was partly due to his belief that he might get medication like Ritalin or Adderal for this. We kept telling him he was normal but just needed to get focused with school work because we believed him capable of accomplishing more. It is clear to me now that Matt was bipolar in high school but had not presented in such a manner that that diagnosis was considered by those treating him.

There are certain mental health disorders that are often associated with drug use. Depression, bipolar disorder, anxiety, and schizophrenia may begin to show themselves in the teen or early college years. In our case, Matt showed signs of depression at the age of 16 but we thought it was a situational response to the event where he was sexually harassed by another student and labeled "gay"—although he clearly did not appear stereotypical of a gay male.

I found evidence of cigarettes and marijuana remnants in his room and he said they helped him feel less anxious. We immediately started him in counseling and treatment for depression. As he continued in high school he kept trying to convince us he was affected by attention deficit disorder (ADD). It was junior and senior year of high school that he began to use substances to make "his brain seems normal." This is also known as self-medication. He was feeling anxiety and felt as though he didn't fit in. Although he was gifted academically and artistically his grades fell, in fact we are amazed that he graduated from high school at all. Other illnesses like eating disorders or autism spectrum disorder may also be associated with drug use.

What follows is a very brief outline of mental health disorders that often coexist with drug use or may actually drive teens to use in an attempt to self medicate.

Adolescent angst:
Hormonal and social changes can make an even tempered teen into a defiant, moody, chronically irritated or angry person. For some of these kids these moods become very intense and need treatment. Adolescence is an unsettling time. Teens want to test the limits and experiment.

Attention Deficit Disorder: (ADD, ADHD)
The main symptoms are impulsivity, inattentiveness and distractibility. This often shows up by early school age. Conservative estimates put the occurrence at 3-5 % of children. Often this is missed and kids began to self medicate with stimulants or cannabis. ADD does not go away at the end of childhood and can persist into adulthood.

Social anxiety:

Signs of social anxiety disorder are social isolation, particularly at school, poor self image fear of negative judgment. Drugs or alcohol may seem to decrease anxious feelings however, tolerance develops and the condition worsens. Social anxiety can mimic shyness so keep a close eye on your teen because this condition is can be extremely serious.

Schizophrenia:

This manifests itself in the late teens and early twenties. Symptoms include hallucinations, paranoia and anxiety. Psychotic symptoms that mimic this disease may be due to drug use. Hallucinations, delusions, paranoia and anxiety indicate serious mental illness. One percent of Americans are affected with this illness.

Depression:

The main symptom of depression may be moodiness, irritability, physical complaints (headaches, stomach aches), sleep problems, or poor grades. One out of ten teens is affected by depression. Teens commonly turn to drug use to self medicate and get rid of negative feelings. Chronic use of drugs can actually amplify their depressed feelings. However, some teens end up with depression because of drug or alcohol use. The risk for depression increases in the teen years. It is estimated that 4-8% of adolescents suffer major depressive disorders, with females at a higher risk than males.

Suicide:

According to the Center for Disease Control (CDC), suicide was the third leading cause of death in 15 to 24 year olds in 2010. This accounts for 12.2% of all deaths annually. In 2009 6.3% of high school students surveyed reported they had attempted suicide in the past 12 months. The use of drugs and alcohol increases the suicide risk for teens.

Post traumatic stress (PTSD):

Kids may show signs of anxiety, depression, self harming thoughts, or actions like cutting. Flashbacks to an event may indicate this disorder. Kids may have been abused, seen a death, or have been involved in a major traumatic event like a car wreck.

Bipolar disorder:

Also known as manic depression because of the shifts in moods that occur, bipolar disorder is a very difficult condition to diagnose because there is a wide range of symptoms and each individual presents differently. Add drug use to the equation and it takes a long time to sort out the symptoms and get a definitive diagnosis. Although signs may be there, many experts feel that bipolar disorder does not fully manifest itself until the age of 12. Kids may have symptoms of irritability, manic moods, alternating with depression or euphoria. Substance abuse is found most often in people who have manic episodes and can change symptoms significantly, Reacting as a Parent to a Diagnosis of Mental Health Conditions

Remember above all you are not alone. There is help out there for you and your child. Parents wonder why this happened and how they could have prevented it. You did not cause your child's mental illness, nor did you cause their drug use. Society in general is becoming more aware of the prevalence of depression as evidenced by the myriad of commercials on TV, and in print for medications to treat depression. But I feel there is still, to a certain degree, a negative view attached to the diagnosis of a mental disorder. Please don't let this affect you. Hold your head up and be proud that you are addressing it for the sake of your child and yourself. It is hard at first to be opened about it but in the openness and in confronting it comes healing.

Although depression and bipolar disorder may run in some families not all children get ill. What you can do is to help your teen cope with their disease and get clean. Abstinence is foremost in helping these kids stabilize. Medical compliance is critical in helping to prevent future drug use. Teens may have trouble remembering to take medications or may rebel at the reality they require medications daily. As a responsible parent, we must be sure they take their medications. Often teens and adults alike will stop using medications because they don't "like how they feel on them." Teens will describe this as a "numb" feeling.

Another issue is that when they begin to feel better they think that they no longer need medication, and the discontinuation of the medication puts them back into the uncontrolled mental state. Helping kids stay generally healthy is critical. Good nutrition, exercise, good sleep habits and relaxation activities are the key. Above all remember that you need to do this as well. Parents need support too. A teen with a psychiatric diagnosis is terrifying! Coping with their mood swings, worrying about the threat of suicide, and making sure they take medications is a daunting task. Guiding them to make good choices, helping them avoid substances, and keeping them away from bad influences is a full time job! It's enough to make you feel crazy, depressed, and anxious yourself.

Keeping your home stable for other siblings is also difficult. The siblings may need counseling as well. You absolutely need emotional support too. Friends, clergy, support groups, counselors are all good resources. A list of National organizations with local chapters and web sites that you might find helpful can be found in the Appendix.

During my journey, I worried a lot and felt off balance. I managed to continue working, taking care of my patients' needs, and ignoring my needs during the day. This helped because for 8 hours a day I was not obsessing on my problems. Somehow I managed to maintain a somewhat "normal" schedule; watching my daughter play soccer, visiting my elderly mother, and maintaining the house. When I was particularly stressed I would scrub the floors. (My family thought I was nuts.) My friends at work and my family watched out for me. My life has been truly blessed by my amazing friends and family.

CHAPTER TWELVE
Legal Issues

"5150---a three day vacation."
~ Matt

If your minor is arrested for drug possession be sure to get an attorney. Adult and juvenile laws are different and juvenile offenses can have far reaching consequences. A juvenile is a minor, under the age of 18. Juvenile court is very powerful and complicated to understand. Lawyers who specialize in juvenile criminal defense may be your best bet. It is critical to understand the options available to your teen. Teens who are arrested are "charged" with violating criminal offenses. The court then has broad control over the life of a minor. Once a teen is arrested, the parents must be notified immediately. Teens over the age of 18 are considered adults and may need a criminal defense attorney.

The Juvenile justice system became U.S. policy in 1899. It was based on the premise that youth were different than adults in their ability to make wise decisions, understand the effects of their action, and comprehend the irrevocable reality of committing a criminal act. Youth were viewed as having a better chance of changing criminal behavior than adults. In addition youth were at risk of being victims of prison violence. In 1974 the Juvenile Justice and Delinquency Prevention Act was instituted which made community based programs available for youth offenders.

There are numerous privately operated websites you can access on line. Many will refer you to the sponsoring attorney or law office of the sponsor.

Matt's arrest
At the time of his arrest for possession of drugs and paraphernalia Matt was 19. He was charged with two potential felonies. These were reduced to misdemeanors.

He saw this as "no big deal" in his drugged state and made light of his night in jail calling it a "study of who is in jail." We bailed him out by posting a $10,000 bond; the cost to us was $1000. We also faced the uncertainty that Matt might disappear making us responsible for the $10,000 bond. We hired a criminal defense attorney; the cost to us was $5000. The attorney was able to get the charges reduced to misdemeanor possession and Matt was placed in a first offender, delayed entry of judgment (DEJ) program.

This meant that if Matt complied with terms of his probation, attended court ordered rehab, and attended 12 step meetings for 18 months, he could have his arrest expunged from his record; in essence a have clean record. Probation and court ordered meetings also had a price tag of about $200 a month. This was touch and go but fortunately after Matt's release from his 4 month rehab program the judge stated, "You have done more than most drug offenders, your charges are dropped." What a relief!

CHAPTER THIRTEEN
Where Do We Go From Here?

"I've had to learn how to control my bipolar disorder and not let it control me. It's a daily struggle, some days I'll want to be alone, sleep all day or not go to work. Other days I feel like everything is fine and perfect and I can accomplish anything. But, it's very tiring."

~ Matt

Matt has just celebrated his eight year drug free anniversary on November 4, 2012. What an amazing accomplishment and we are very proud of Matt! Now 28, Matt is very stable mentally. Although doing well, Matt knows that he can never let his guard down or become complacent about his diseases. Our family has regained a balance of sorts. With that said, we know things can change.

We are here to support Matt as he continues in his life journey. That doesn't mean we as parents feel entirely free of worry about relapse though. Relapse is common for addicts. Matt says the main reason he relapsed before going to his 4 month rehab was because of the people he continued to hang out with. He said he would be clean for a week but his dealers would look him up and give him free drugs and it would start all over.

I have been asked by others going through this with their teen, what about setbacks? It seems during the intense part of recovery positive steps are made only to be followed by set backs. I saw this as 2 steps forward followed by 6 steps backwards. This feels devastating when it happens. Feelings of hopelessness and feeling extremely overwhelmed are common during recovery while you are trying to re-balance your life and family dynamics. I can only encourage you to continue on and take one day at a time. Your kid and your sanity are worth fighting for!

Look for emotional and professional support. You may find it in surprising and unusual places. I have wonderful friends that stuck by me through all the craziness. My colleagues at work, church friends, and neighbors were there as well. My family physician was a rock of support. I spent many hours on the Internet looking for information and yes expert advice is out there if you just search. I went to NAMI meetings, co-dependent meetings, individual counseling, and family support groups. I have shared my story every chance I get and heard other stories far worse than my own.

My words of advice are, "DON'T GIVE UP." Take one day at a time and you will eventually get to where you and your teen are suppose to be. Good luck in your journey.

"I'm a victor at the end of the day by not scratching the itch an addict can so easily scratch and by learning to manage my bipolar disorder.
I know that if I can rise above these obstacles and find peace within myself, the creativity that's somewhere lost inside will reemerge."

~ Matt

Epilogue

As I was readying this book for publication I did a lot of reflecting on the past. Although, reliving it might be a better description. One surprising thing happened. I began to have many of the old feelings that were so very uncomfortable during the intense parts of Matt's and my recovery. I think this reinforces the notion that you never really forget the past feelings of being the parent of a drug abuser and the worries that relapse of your loved one might happen again is a reality. My best friend agrees. She also worries about her adult son who had very minor issues compared to Matt. I guess that's what being a parent is all about. Recovery from drug abuse is not guaranteed.

So, feeling overwhelmed with these old feelings, I went to Matt and asked him if he is really ok. All I managed to do was to make both of us crazy in the process. He did reassure me that life is good and he has no desire to use. I guess I was looking for absolute reassurance that I need not worry. The reality is that there is no absolute resolution. I believe to gain acceptance and peace, faith and hope must be at work here. Matt's response is, "Mom those feelings are your issues, not mine and at you need to work on those." How true.

I remember while Matt was in rehab after his assigned time on toilet duty was over, he was assigned to the kitchen detail. The manager of the kitchen was a kind woman who recognized the goodness in Matt and kept reminding him that deep down he was a good kid. She always took the time during our weekly visits to reassure me that the good Matt was beginning to show. She said it was evident that we had "raised him right" because this began to show as he progressed in his recovery. Although not a counselor, Eleanor had a big part in Matt's recovery as he began to remember who he was and where he came from. This was very helpful to me because I received affirmation that my husband and I had been good parents and had indeed done some things right! I encourage you to remember the good things about your child.

Matt attends college and is close to an Associate's degree in fine art from our local community college with the hopes of becoming a graphic designer or print maker. He finds joy and solace in working with his art. He has also been employed for 7 years by the same company he started with one year after his time in rehab. His bipolar disorder is stable and he has continuously taken his medications without a single lapse.

Matt has recently weathered 3 major storms. The first was the death of his beloved Paco, the family dog, whom we adopted when Matt was 16 and starting into his depression. Paco was his therapy dog. Early in his recovery I asked him what might precipitate a relapse and he replied, "I guess if Paco died." Matt was sad but put Paco's death into perspective and moved on. Another was the breakup of a significant relationship with a woman that lasted a year and a half. He came through this (not without my worrying) with a new maturity.

Also during the past year my 91 year old mother pasted away. Matt was always very close to her. I remember the last time he saw her was during one of her final lucid moments. Mom had sunk into the depths of dementia. On the day of our visit, she awoke from a nap and saw Matt, and her beautiful Irish smile lit up her often vacant

face. She grinned, hugged him, and as he lay next to her on her bed for a while, her first words to him were, "What are those things in your ears?" She had to bug him about his large ear plugs one last time. Laughter followed and she told him she loved him, held his hand for a while and went back to sleep. I have a great picture of this moment and cherish the memory.

I am not sure what pulled me through this horrible time in my life. I know faith had a big part; I trusted that the Lord would help us through this challenge. I also held on to the belief of hope; hope for a good outcome for Matt.

I know faith, hope, trust, and resiliency were the keys to my recovery. Resiliency was something I didn't know I had until I read an article in my Sunday paper a few weeks ago. Please keep in mind that you can learn to be resilient. It is not a genetic thing that you have or don't. No two people react to the trauma of teen substance abuse in the same manner. Life challenges in ways we never dreamed are possible. Set backs are a part of life.

We have to learn to bounce back. Social support is essential and I was blessed to have family and friends to keep me sane. Knowing there is someone to count on is essential. Outlook is important as well. I have always been more optimistic than pessimistic. Optimism helps you to filter out negative thoughts that do not always reflect the reality of the situation. Pessimism is contagious. There were times I felt things were pretty much hopeless during Matt's treatment. That's when I relied on my faith and hope for a good outcome. Other factors that contribute to resiliency are flexibility, core value system, faith, positive role models, physical fitness, cognitive strength, facing fears, and most importantly finding meaning in life struggles.

There is a psychological concept called "locus of control." I learned about this as a college student. This has helped guide me through life. An individual with internal locus of control believes that their behavior is guided by personal decisions and efforts, rather than believing that external forces such as fate, luck or other circumstances control behavior. Although my life was pretty much out of control during Matt's drug use, I knew deep down that my decisions and efforts could have an effect on a positive outcome.

I am still working as a Women's Health Specialist at a University in Los Angeles. I believe that one of the purposes of my struggles with Matt was to help me identify students with issues. By sharing Matt's story I can connect with some of my patients on a different level and help them recognize that they might need help with mental health or substance use issues.

Finding meaning in life's struggles is important and I believe that as a result of my struggles, I was meant to tell Matt's story to help families with a teen substance abuse problem. This book started taking shape one year after Matt got clean. The story is not over we just continue experience new "chapters" as a recovering family.

Here is a family update.

MATT

"If some one asked me in the year 2003 where I thought I'd be in 5 years, my answer would have been dead. I was on a path of destruction heading to my demise, until my world got turned upside down. In this game of life we are on a continual journey of learning. I have learned many lessons along the way. After completing my four month stay at rehab in 2004 I have continued to stay off dope. I may be clean at this point of time but I know I will live the rest of my life as an addict at heart. Though addiction played a big roll in my downward spiral, the main problem was my bipolar disorder which I still struggle with on a daily basis. Through the support of family, friends, and doctors as well as the proper medication I can continue to maintain my sobriety and live a normal nine to five life. I now know for a fact that without the support of my family, through my journey to get clean I would not have succeeded like I have.

One thing I have now, that I never even thought about before, is establishing goals and having ambitions. The one thing that has held me together through all my hard times is my love of art. This love has manifested into a passion and I know that I was destined to make a career out of my love for creating visually stimulating works of art. I am currently in school pursuing my undergraduate studies in fine art and I ultimately want to get a MFA. Though not knowing exactly what career I want to pursue after finishing school I, have narrowed it down to some where in the illustration, graphic design, or printmaking fields.

Looking back on all that has happen to me, I wouldn't change a thing. Some may ask after hearing my story, why? The reason for this is I believe that everything we experience molds us into the person we are. The saying "Whatever doesn't kill you, makes you stronger" is more than just a saying, it is the truth. I hope that I can share my wisdom from my life experiences. If I can positively influence just one individual and encourage them to change, then all my trials and tribulations will have been worth it."

GUY - Matt's Father
Then Now and Future

"It is my honor to add a few thoughts to Matt's story. Our son, Matthew Robert Gilchrist is a Miracle. As his father I have had the privilege of witnessing his continued transformation. I watched Matt, an angry, self indulging, insecure boy/young man state he was "dumb and could not learn." This boy/man revealed to me that he lied, stole, and dealt to buy his drugs and only cared about where he would get his next fix. He was a boy/man doomed to end up in prison or die from a drug overdose.

I now see Matt, the man, changed into a compassionate, intelligent, loving, purposeful man who works 30 hours a week while successfully attending college full time as he pursues a curriculum in which he is truly gifted. I now see my son, Matt, clean for 8 years, 1 month and 27 days from the use of speed to go up and heroin to come down. As I watched Matt, the miracle, unfold I came to know that only a power greater than ourselves could have made this transformation possible. I, as a man who had pursued the idols of this world for most of my adult life, through the Miracle of Matt, I was able to accept Jesus Christ as My Lord and Savior in August 2006. Do I still make mistakes? Unquestionably. Do I know I am forgiven? Absolutely. Am I growing to be a father, husband and a good man? Definitely! Matt has been instrumental in opening my eyes and most importantly my heart and I will always be grateful! Matt not only do I love you, you are my son and I am exceedingly well pleased."

MEGAN - Matt's Sister

Megan graduated from college in 2009. Medical school is in her future. Megan plans to be a surgeon. She has come to accept and understand Matt's disorder. She is currently working at a major cancer research hospital in Los Angeles where she is involved with brain and breast cancer projects. She was a high school senior when Matt's illness hit. The family stress was extreme but she managed to graduate with honors and was accepted at several prestigious colleges. Living away at college helped separate her from the craziness of our home. Matt and Megan are again friends and share a love of sushi.

Appendix

RESOURCES

During my search for information I found the best and most current information came from the internet. What follows are the sites that helped me to gain insight and understanding of Matthew's journey.

TEENS:

http://www.Freevibe.com
> Youth oriented information
> Office of National Drug Control Policy

http://www.whatsyourantidrug.com/
> National youth media campaign from the Office of National Drug Control Policy

http://www.NIDA.NIH.gov/students.html
> A site for teens emphasizing grades five through nine

http://www.abovetheinfluence.comut
> Videos for teens about drug use and making good choices

PARENTS:

http://www.ncfy.com/publicationa
> National Clearing House on Families and Youth.
> Supporting your Adolescent: Tips for Parents

http://timetoact.drugfree.org/
> Partnership for Drug Free America. This is a tool for parents which uses videos and scenarios and helps parents determine a plan of action is they suspect or know their child is using drugs

http://www.toosmarttostart.samhsa.gov/Start.aspx

http://www.teenhelp.com

A website for parents, teens, educators which provides many resources on parenting teens, troubled teens and treatment. Also tips for teens

http://www.EROWID.org

Online library

A member supported origination "providing access to reliable nonjudgmental information about psychotropic plants and chemical and related issues.

http://www.tnpc.com

Articles on teens from the McCall's Magazine Publisher

http://www.parents.com

A site for parents sponsored by publishers of Parent, Child, Family Circle and McCall's magazines

http://www.PRIDEyouthprograms.org/

Resources for parents

http://www.talkingwithkids.org

Resources, organizations, websites and book

MENTAL HEALTH

http://www.AACAP.org

American Academy of Child and Adolescent Psychiatry

http://nimh.nih.gov

National Institute of Mental Health

http://www.SAMHSA.gov/

Substance Abuse and Mental Health Services Administration

http://www.dbsalliance.org

Depression and Bipolar Support Alliance

http://www.AAP.org

American Academy of Pediatrics

http://www.Collegedrinkingprevention.gov

College drinking changing the culture, a government website which gives statistics and information about college drinking behaviors

http://www.nationaleatingdisorders.org/

National Eating Disorders Association

http://www.niaaa.nih.gov/

National Institute on Alcohol Abuse and Alcoholism

SEXUAL HEALTH

http://www.ashastd.org

American Social Health Association
General information about sexually transmitted diseases

GENERAL DRUG INFORMATION

http://www.nih.gov/

National Institute of Health

http://www.hhs.gov/

U.S. Department of Health and Human Services

http://www.drugabuse.gov/

National Institute on Drug Abuse

http://www.justice.gov/dea/index.shtml

Drug Enforcement Agency

http:/www.sadd.org

Students Against Destructive Decisions
Students helping students make good choices

http://www.samhsa.gov/

Substance Abuse and Mental Health Services Administration

http://www.uclaisap.org/

UCLA Integrative Substance Abuse Program
Research training and treatment information

http://www.methamphetamine.org

Information about methamphetamines

http://www.al-anon.org/

Al-Anon and Alateen

http://www.niaaa.nih.gov/

National Institute on Alcohol Abuse and Alcoholism

http://www.whitehousedrugpolicy.gov

Publications on national policy

http://www.ncadd.org

National Council on Alcoholism and Drug Dependence

Advocates for children and families affected by alcoholism

http://www.nacoa.org

National association for children of alcoholics

LEGAL

Office of Juvenile Justice and Delinquency Prevention

http://www.ncjj.org/

National Center for Juvenile Justice

http://ncjrs.gov/

National Criminal Justice Reference Service

ADOLESCENT DEVELOPMENT

Web MD Health General Information

Search growth and development

http://mail.prideyouthprograms.org/

Parents Resource Institute for Drug Education

http://www.talkingwithkids.org

Resources, organizations websites and books

Chapter References

Chapter 4:

Hardiman, Michael. Overcoming Addiction. The Crossing Press: California. 2000.
Page 36

Ruden, Ronald A. The Craving Brain. Second Edition. Perennial: New York. 2000
Pages 18-19, 61-62

NIIDA Info facts: Lessons from Prevention Research

Chapter 5

Ruden pages 43-53

Chapter 6

Hardiman pages 9-21, 88
AMA Counsel on Scientific Affairs Task Force of the Panel on Alcoholism and Drug Abuse. 2000

NIDA booklet, "Drugs, brains and behavior. The science of addiction."

Chapter 7

NIDA Info Facts: High school and Youth Trend
Teenhelp.com
Monitoring the Future 2008

Chapter 8

NIDA (National Institute on Drug Abuse)

Chapter 9

National Center on Addiction and Substance Abuse

American Lung Association

National Highway Traffic Safety Administration

Chapter 10

NIDA Research Report Series-Hallucinogens and Dissociative Drugs 7-22-08

Department of Justice Office of diversion control

DEA 2002 enforcement Agency

Substance Abuse and Mental Health Services Administration (SAMSA)

Chapter 14

National Institute on Drug Abuse

National Survey of Drug Use and Health 2005

Lecture: Angela Golden "Problems in California and the Southwest: Meth-amphetamines" Presented at CANP Annual Meeting San Diego March 2008

Chapter16

NIDA

Up to Date.com

American Society of Addiction

American Academy of Addiction Psychiatry

Chapter 18

Children and Adults with Attention Deficit/Hyperactive Disorder (CHADD)

American Academy of Child and Adolescent Psychology

Up to Date ;Teen Depression

Center for Disease Control

Chapter19

Lawyer Shop Family Law and Personal Injury Directory (Free advice website)

Contact Information

Donna can be reached at dbgilchrist@aol.com

Proceeds from the book will be used to finance Matthew's college education.

About The Author

Donna Beard Gilchrist is the mother of a recovering junkie. She is a very successful Nurse Practitioner with over 35 years of patient care experience. Donna is a Board Certified Women's Health Nurse Practitioner. She completed her BSN, Bachelor of Science in Nursing, at California State University, Long Beach. She attended graduate school at California State University Los Angeles where she completed her MSN, Masters of Science in Nursing. Her clinical training as a Nurse practitioner was completed in the Kaiser Permanente-CSULA training program in 1975.

Donna practiced at Kaiser Permanente in Southern California for 35 years, retired and is currently in her eighth year of practice as a College Health Nurse Practitioner at University of Southern California. She has been a visiting instructor to a California State University.

Donna also taught for many years in a Nurse Practitioner Educational Program. She has been a speaker at numerous continuing education programs for Nurse Practitioners and Physician Assistants. In addition to her current college health practice, Donna has become a popular speaker on campus to student groups about how to stay healthy while attending college. Donna was blind sided when she discovered that her teenage son was a substance abuser and feels her new mission is to tell parents her story of hope and success.

About Dr. Bradley Meier, author of Book Foreword

Dr. Bradley Meier is a licensed psychologist who currently lives and practices in Los Angeles. For more than a dozen years he provided services, administrated addiction treatment programs, and performed faculty duties for the Department of Psychiatry at Thomas Jefferson University in Philadelphia. He has published and presented on the topic of addiction and had a primary role in starting the first dual diagnosis In-patient program for the state hospital in Delaware.

Currently he is the Director of Counseling on the Health Science Campus of the University of Southern California and has a private psychology practice in downtown Los Angeles.

About John Martin - Smokefade SM Creator

John E. Martin, Ph.D.is a licensed clinical psychologist and addiction and motivation expert who has served on the faculties of the following Universities and Medical Schools and Centers: VA Medical Center (Jackson, Miss) (Staff Psychologist, Director of Smoking Clinic and Behavioral Medicine Program) – 1978-1986; University of Mississippi Medical Center (Assistant and Associate Professor of Psychiatry and Medicine; 1978-86); San Diego State University (Professor of Psychology, 1986-2006); University of California, San Diego, School of Medicine (Associate Adjunct Professor of Psychiatry; Program Co-Director and Director of Clinical Training, SDSU/UCSD Joint Doctoral Program in Clinical Psychology, 1988-1990); Fuller Graduate School of Psychology (Professor of Clinical Psychology, 2007-2010).

Dr. Martin has published over 70 articles in scientific journals, two books and many book chapters, including over 100 professional presentations at scientific organizations. He has received more than $2 million in federal and state of Calif grants in the areas of addictions, smoking, and health and disease risk modification. He has been on the editorial boards and review boards of numerous scientific journals, including national VA and NIH grant review boards